Paths of Individuation
in Literature and Film

Paths of Individuation in Literature and Film

A Jungian Approach

Phyllis Berdt Kenevan

LEXINGTON BOOKS
Lanham • Boulder • New York • Oxford

LEXINGTON BOOKS

Published in the United States of America
by Lexington Books
4720 Boston Way, Lanham, Maryland 20706

12 Hid's Copse Road
Cumnor Hill, Oxford OX2 9JJ, England

Copyright © 1999 by Lexington Books

All rights reserved. No part of this publication may be reproduced,
stored in a retrieval system, or transmitted in any form or by any
means, electronic, mechanical, photocopying, recording, or otherwise,
without the prior permission of the publisher.

British Library Cataloguing in Publication Information Available

Library of Congress Cataloging-in-Publication Data

Kenevan, Phyllis B.
    Paths of individuation in literature and film : a Jungian approach
/ Phyllis Berdt Kenevan
      p. cm.
    Includes bibliographical references and index.
    ISBN 0-7391-0016-5 (cloth)
    1. Motion pictures—Psychological aspects. 2. Motion pictures and
literature. 3. Individuation (Psychology) I. Title.
PN1995.K43 1999
791.43'01'9—dc21   99-11559
                                                  CIP

Printed in the United States of America

∞™ The paper used in this publication meets the minimum requirements of American
National Standard for Information Sciences—Permanence of Paper for Printed Library
Materials, ANSI Z39.48–1992.

To Peter and Bridget

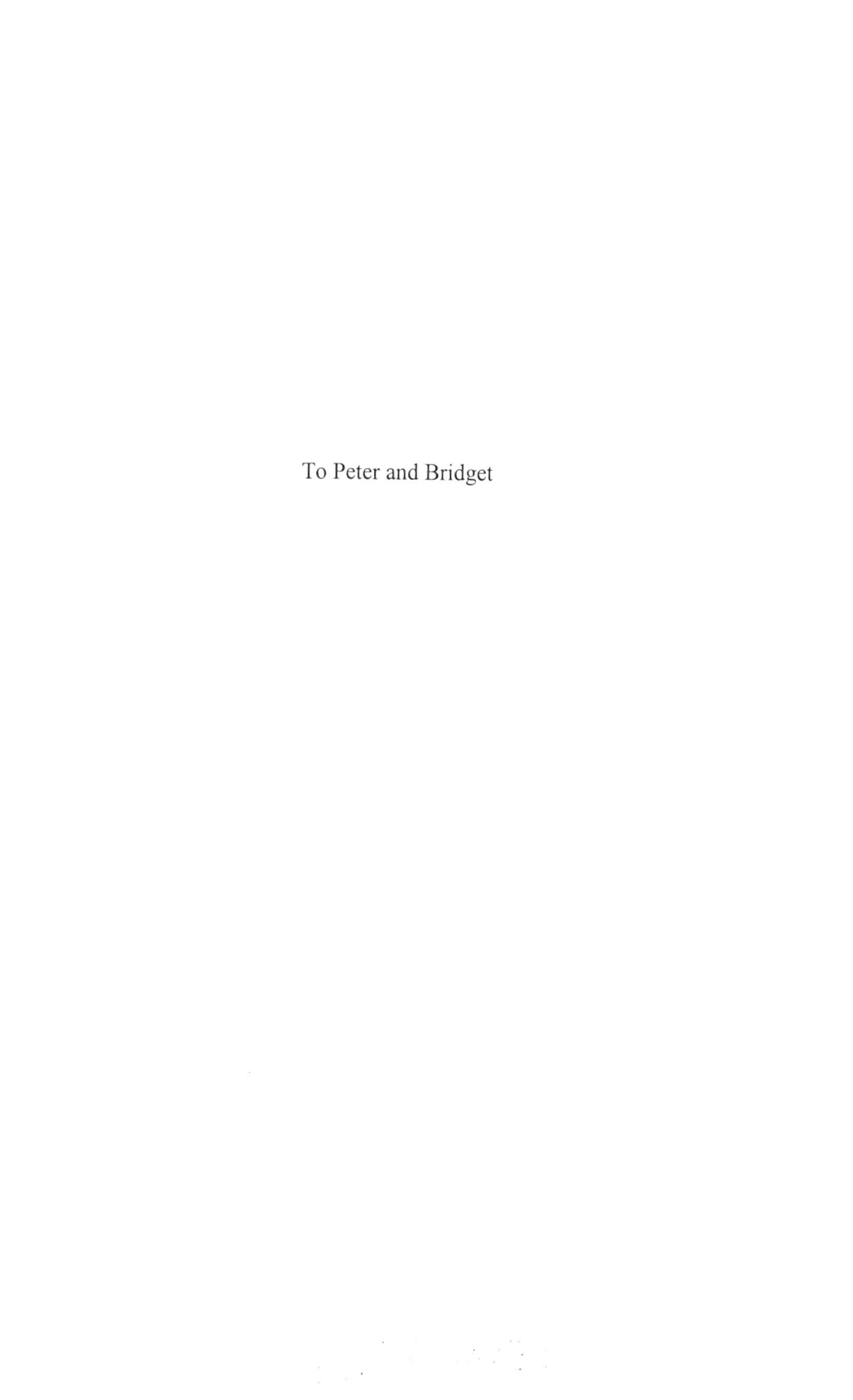

CONTENTS

Acknowledgments		ix
Introduction		1

PART ONE: INDIVIDUAL PATHS

Chapter 1	Nature's Gift: The Individuation of an Ogre *Zorba the Greek*	13
Chapter 2	An Anima Run Amok *The House of the Spirits*	29
Chapter 3	A Reluctant Victim of Individuation *Crime and Punishment*	43
Chapter 4	The Rainmaker of Bagdad *Bagdad Cafe*	57

PART TWO: COLLECTIVE PATHS

Chapter 5	The Life of the Spirit in Modern Man: Feast or Famine? *My Dinner With André*	71
Chapter 6	Rebirth, Prophecy, and the Big Dream Novels of Dostoyevsky	83
Chapter 7	Where Angels Dare to Tread *Wings of Desire*	97

Bibliography	117
Index	121
About the Author	125

ACKNOWLEDGMENTS

For reading the entire manuscript with care and for her many helpful suggestions, I am grateful to Linda Schierse Leonard. I also thank Jean Thyfault for her reading and criticism of the manuscript, and Charles Kenevan and Ann Ashley Miller for their reading, their suggestions, and their help in so many ways. For also reading the manuscript and for their support and encouragement, I thank Hazel Barnes and Doris Schwalbe. I owe a special thanks and recognition to Barbara S. Farnsworth for the many hours she put in proofreading and preparing the manuscript, and to Luzie Mason who, in completing the final copy, found and helped me to correct several potential grammatical confusions. Preda Mihailescu I thank for his generous hospitality during my 1989 spring semester in Zürich and Küsnacht, and I also thank the publishers who granted me permission to quote from the following works:

Knowing Woman, by Irene Claremont de Castillejo. Copyright © 1973 by the C. G. Jung Foundation for Analytical Psychology. Reprinted by arrangement with Shambhala Publications, Inc.

Zorba the Greek, by Nikos Kazantzakis, trans. Carl Wildman. Copyright © 1953 and 1981 by Simon & Schuster, Inc. Reprinted by permission of Simon & Schuster, Inc.

From Conversations with C. G. Jung, by Margaret Ostrowski-Sachs. Printed by Juris Druck + Verlag AG, Zürich, 1971 and 1977. Reprinted by permission of the C. G. Jung-Institut, Zürich.

Bagdad Cafe, by Eleonore Adlon and Percy Adlon. Copyright © 1987 by pelemele FILM GmbH production. Reprinted by permission of pelemele PICTURES, Inc.

The House of the Spirits, by Isabel Allende, trans. M. Bogin. Copyright © 1985 by Alfred A. Knopf, Inc. Reprinted by permission of the publisher.

A Raw Youth, by Fyodor Dostoyevsky, trans. Constance Garnett. Copyright © 1947 by the Dial Press, Inc. Reprinted with the permission of

Simon & Schuster from *A Raw Youth* by Fyodor Dostoevsky, translated from the Russian by Constance Garnett (New York: Macmillan, 1923).

Quotes from *My Dinner With André*, by Wallace Shawn and André Gregory. Copyright © 1981 by Wallace Shawn and André Gregory. Used with permission of Grove/Atlantic, Inc.

Modern Man in Search of a Soul, by C. G. Jung. Copyright © 1933 by Harcourt Brace and World, Inc. Reprinted by permission of Harcourt Brace & Company.

Jung, Carl Gustav, *Civilization in Transition vol. 10, Collected Works, Second Edition.* Copyright © 1975 by Princeton University Press. Reprinted by permission of Princeton University Press.

Jung, Carl Gustav, *C. G. Jung Speaking.* Copyright © 1977 by Princeton University Press. Reprinted by permission of Princeton University Press.

Jung, Carl Gustav, *Psychological Reflections.* Copyright © 1974 by Princeton University Press. Reprinted by permission of Princeton University Press.

Jung, Carl Gustav, *Two Essays on Analytical Psychology.* Copyright © 1967 by Princeton University Press. Reprinted by permission of Princeton University Press.

INTRODUCTION

Spiritual Nihilism

It is hardly news that we live in a troubled world, that we are haunted by nihilism, that we have even become bored with the reiteration that we live in a spiritual vacuum. Nietzsche's madman who rushed into the market place—ahead of his time—and who dashed his lantern on the ground in despair over the failure of his listeners to acknowledge his warning of the death of God,[1] and thereby of our whole moral order, was fortunate in at least one respect. He did not have to live through the confirmation of his predictions.

The "shadows of God," our increasingly obsolete canons of morality, he warned, would haunt us until their exposure as groundless would leave us in both personal and collective disorder. With no "up or down," we would be compelled to stray through an "infinite nothing" in all directions—an apt description of our modern confusion in regard to our collective judgments about abortion, capital punishment, social justice, civil rights, health care, ecology, corruption in business and politics, the military, war and peace.

The moral failures of our time are also evident in the lack of idealism in young college-age students who no longer look upon the professions, for example, law, medicine or government, as giving meaning and value. Instead they seem to be polarizing between those who look only for the financial rewards and those who try to give value to their lives through crusades for minority rights, gay and lesbian movements, feminist issues, and the growing environmentalist movement.

Even though Nietzsche's madman may have come too early, his warning appears to have reached us too late. Today we are so deeply embedded in that breakdown of old values that we have to a large extent embraced nihilism as the norm. In fact, "the spiritual problem of modern man" may be precisely that we are no longer aware that we have a spiritual problem, or that there might be a way out of nihilism.

One who was acutely aware of the problem, however, was C. G. Jung, the Swiss depth psychologist who encountered the spiritual problem again and again among his patients, and who gradually came to the realization that "danger itself fosters the rescuing power;"[2] that the way out of spiritual emptiness was not to be found in a restless external search but in an inner journey to one's own depths, from which one could be led to a new wholeness of body, mind and spirit. This goal of wholeness, of finding the total Self, took on the character of a new spiritual quest, in the process of which an increasing fascination with the unconscious filled the gap of metaphysical loss.

> Whenever there exists some external form, be it an ideal or a ritual, by which all the yearnings and hopes of the soul are adequately expressed—as for instance in a living religion—then we may say the psyche is outside and that there is no psychic problem, just as there is then no unconscious in our sense of the word. In consonance with this truth, the discovery of psychology falls entirely within the last decades, although long before that man was introspective and intelligent enough to recognize the facts that are the subject-matter of psychology.[3]

In Jung's view, the preoccupation with psychology, so predominant in our time, is an indication that we expect something from the psyche that we have not found in the outer world, something which our religion ought to contain but no longer does. That failure of religion to provide guidance and the absence of an unambiguous collective moral canon, he claimed, brought more and more preoccupation with the psychological; for when people could no longer find guidance from collective norms to help them resolve personal moral dilemmas, they turned increasingly to the psychoanalyst or psychologist for help.

Jung's trust in the unconscious as a healing and creative source, together with the corollary that reason, or our consciousness, represents only a limited side of us, has made his position for some people a controversial one. The dethronement of reason as sole reliable guide does not mean, however, that a mystical unconscious has been deified in its place, for although he advocates that symbolic messages from the unconscious are to be taken seriously, he never advocated that they be taken as oracles. It is the integration of conscious and unconscious that is crucial for Jung, and that involves both an openness to the unconscious and a critical intelligence. Both are needed because as our personal and collective lives become more and more complex, the need for a deeper self-knowledge and moral integrity becomes

INTRODUCTION

imperative. Jung referred to our age in terms of what the Greeks called "the right moment for a metamorphosis of the gods." He saw this moment as synonymous with the emergence in our time of the unconscious, which becomes a source of spiritual transformation, perhaps even spiritual evolution. Jung claimed a reluctance to take the role of prophet, preferring to leave it to us whether we see decadence or transformation in the future; nevertheless, he predicted transformation through the presence of psychic forces.

> The effect on *all* individuals, which one would like to see realized, may not set in for hundreds of years, for the spiritual transformation of mankind follows the slow tread of the centuries and cannot be hurried or held up by any rational process of reflection, let alone brought to fruition in one generation. What does lie within our reach, however, is the change in individuals who have, or create for themselves, an opportunity to influence others of like mind.[4]

The slow path to this transformation of humankind he saw as a process which could only happen through the struggle of individuals to find their own ways toward their own unique wholeness. He called this spiritual journey "the path of individuation."

Individuation

It was because of his discovery that the assimilation of unconscious contents into an integrated whole had remarkable effects upon ego-consciousness that Jung came to see it as the possibility of spiritual transformation.

> That we find it needful to draw analogies from psycho-pathology and from both Eastern and Western mysticism is only to be expected: the individuation process is, psychically, a borderline phenomenon which needs special conditions in order to become conscious. Perhaps it is the first step along a path of development to be trodden by the men of the future.[5]

More specifically, then, what did Jung mean by individuation? All living things, he claimed, tended toward a goal, and just as the acorn is intended to become an oak, so we are by nature intended for our own full development. Just as not all acorns become oak trees, however, not all of us achieve our potential as integrated human beings. Jung's method of analytical psychology is aimed at facilitating that process. Although individuation is not something one *attains* once and for all, it is always before us as a goal toward which we strive, some being more successful in this pursuit than others. An individuated person is one who has fulfilled potentials, integrated both conscious and unconscious sides of himself, and learned to live from the total psyche instead of identifying himself only with the conscious ego. Jung calls this transformation a process of recentering from ego to Self. Since we cannot transcend our consciousness, we cannot *know* our Self, but we can live from that larger center by becoming cognizant of ourselves as more than our consciousness and taking seriously the motivation and symbolic messages that come from the unconscious. This sort of openness or awareness is what Jung called listening to the Voice.

Normally, says Jung, the unconscious collaborates with the conscious without friction or disturbance. When we deviate too far from our instinctual foundations, however, we soon experience the full impact of unconscious forces. Since the collaboration of the unconscious is intelligent and purposive, even when it acts in opposition to consciousness, its expression is still compensatory, as if it were trying to restore the lost balance.

Jung's account of the unconscious psyche goes backward and forward. Immensely old, it is also capable of growing into an equally remote future; but the goal of psychic development remains always the Self, which is reached not through any linear evolution, but through a process Jung called a "circumambulation" of the Self. It is the Self as organizing center or inner director which guides the maturing of the personality, sending its symbolic messages through the inner Voice to the ego. Whether or not the ego is willing to listen to these messages will determine how completely that person will reach the goal of individuation. If the ego listens to that inner urge to growth, the uniqueness of that person will be realized even though the Self doing the guiding will never be known.

The concept of individuation, development of the self into an integrated whole, is not a new idea; among others, Nietzsche expressed the same idea when he said, "dare to become who you are." But how do we know who we are? Jung made this ideal more accessible by giving us a language through which we can begin to differentiate ourselves and others and a cast of archetypes in our personal dramas which gave us a handle on what is there to be integrated. From that point of view, it doesn't matter whether his typology and his archetypes are final or absolute description. They give access and form to the integration process and allow us to arrive at some understanding of others and of ourselves. Jung himself said more than once that he was not holding these categories as dogmas. The terms "anima" and "animus," for instance, have become controversial for some people, but whether or not those terms are used is unimportant; the concept of repressed contrasexual characteristics that keep us from reaching an integrated wholeness remains significant. As long as our culture differentiates psychological characteristics in sexual terms, and we conform—in whatever varying degrees—to that culture, what Jung described will be operational. Should we ever arrive at a time when we have a uni-sex society (in terms of psychological characteristics), then the contrasexual interpretation of character formation would no longer be applicable. The same reasoning can be brought to Jung's description of personality types as a guide to understanding the character of others as well as ourselves. No one, Jung has repeatedly warned, is a pure type. The descriptions of thinking, feeling, intuiting, or sensing types are abstractions. Nevertheless people do tend—on the whole—to have differentiated or developed one function more than the others, and so our understanding of that person can be enhanced when we understand the orientation of that type. The difference between the attitude types, extraversion and introversion, works the same way. According to Jung, anyone who was always one or the other would only be found in an asylum. We are, all of us, both types; yet we tend, at least during certain periods of our lives, to be responding to life in one way more than another.

One archetype, however, seems less flexible than the others, and that is the one Jung called the "shadow." The shadow is a name for the personal unconscious which consists of all our consciously rejected characteristics, as well as the undeveloped and therefore primitive aspects of our character. The things we reject about ourselves—those in conflict with our ethical and other ideals— become repressed and, although they still motivate our behavior, we fail to recognize them as such. Instead, we project them on others, a tactic that has moral implications in our private as well as collective lives. That is why Jung claimed that encountering our shadow leaves us with a moral problem. Once aware of what we had repressed, we must deal with it, assimilate it in some acceptable way.

These categories, psychological type, anima, animus, and shadow, all figure predominantly in the four chapters of Part One. In these chapters are four different paths toward the goal of individuation, where psychological type makes a difference in how a character develops. This is particularly the case with Zorba of *Zorba the Greek*, and with Raskolnikov in *Crime and Punishment*. Zorba is a feeling type, whereas Raskolnikov is a captive of his own overvaluation of the intellect. With those differences their paths to self-development go in opposite directions, following the dictates of their original dispositions.

The development of Trueba in *The House of the Spirits*, however, is revealed more readily through a focus upon his relationship with women, as the outer expression of a repressed anima. The gradual and belated integration of that contrasexual side is at the same time the path he takes toward individuation.

Bagdad Cafe evoked yet another archetype, an uncommon one, but one which seemed to best characterize Jasmin and to explain how her individuation produced the charismatic effect she had on those around her. The Rainmaker is a type who initiates the individuation of others by her sheer presence among them.

All four, in their different ways, describe the individuation process as a personal achievement. The three chapters of Part Two, in contrast, are a portrayal of that process in the collective, where the individuation of humanity as a whole is an evolutionary goal. In contrasting the personal and collective, Jung claimed that, while in individual cases transformation can be read from dreams and fantasies, in collective life "it has left its deposit principally in the various religious systems and their changing symbols." He also claimed, as a recurrent theme, that contemporary life is characterized by a spiritual crisis, due to the failure of contemporary religions to provide appropriate symbols. At the same time, he thought that we were perhaps at the threshold of a new spiritual epoch. The three chapters of Part Two rest upon that assumption.

The film *My Dinner With André* focuses upon the inner turmoil of André, who not only recognizes but lives that crisis in his own life. It is the spiritual crisis of modern man that dominates his life and which he tries to resolve through the unorthodox experiences in which he engages himself. He does not resolve those problems in his own life or for the collective, but he does articulate them with courage and honesty.

In the chapter on Dostoyevsky's novels, which focus on what Jung called the Big Dream—dreams which have collective significance—an awakening to the life of the spirit is suggested, but only as a dream of future life. Dostoyevsky, also troubled by the spiritual problem of modern man, suggests that a future evolution of the spirit will come as an inevitable psychological process (an idea that can also be found in Jung), and he defends the need to keep that ideal alive at least as a prophecy.

It is only with the last chapter, an analysis of the film *Wings of Desire*, that a more concrete image is offered for the evolution of humankind, presented in the form of a contemporary myth. The merging of angel and human is the mythic image or symbol for a renewal of humanity, one which does away with our present divorce between spirit and matter. With that union humanity can begin anew; it is a new beginning and a new childhood of humankind.

Although each chapter is an investigation of a separate work, the theme of individuation links them all together; and the collective evolution of Part Two unifies them in a common goal.

Why Literature and Film?

In *The Divided Self*, R. D. Laing tells about a young woman who changed the direction of her life after watching repeated sessions of the film *La Strada*.[6] She told Laing that she saw, in the character of Gelsemina, a reproach to herself for the attitudes she had been holding and the life she had been leading, and with that new insight into her own failure, she experienced a sort of conversion—what Plato called "a turning of the soul," and what, in more contemporary terms, we call a transformative experience. That experience turned her away from what was a pre-psychotic condition toward a more healthy direction.

Her reaction to the film was a more dramatic one than most of us could claim; nevertheless, we all experience to some extent that feeling of significance when a film or a novel makes us aware of something in ourselves that wants to come to the surface. Sometimes we are only aware of a mildly obsessive preoccupation with the work; we may want to see the film again, or talk with someone about a novel. Sometimes we can become almost compulsive in our reaction, for example, a woman sees the film *Reds* nine times; or a man discovers a new writer and buys two more copies which he thrusts upon his friends so that he can discuss the novel with them; or, leaving the cinema after seeing *Gandhi*, a man discovers in himself a powerful renewal of the idealism he believed long since vanquished by the practical demands of everyday life; or a young woman, turning the last page of a D. H. Lawrence novel, wonders if she should break her engagement.

These personal responses to literature and film reflect a form of communication that reaches us on more than one level. It seems that, while we are outwardly mere spectators of the film or silent readers of the novel, an inner observer is relating itself to the characters, situation, action, and reacting to the work in highly personal ways. In this respect, novels and films are also like our dreams or fantasies; they bring to our conscious awareness messages from an unconscious depth which find expression through the symbols and metaphors of the work.

When we recognize ourselves in the characters and situations of the novel or film, we become receptive to what we otherwise fail to see as belonging to us. For example, a woman who refuses to recognize the signs of increasing rejection by a lover may have no difficulty seeing that situation in the action of the film; and, along with that unresisting recognition of the story unfolding before her eyes, the inner observer's voice slips in . . . "but that is what is happening to you." In that way, a bit of awareness comes to consciousness through the medium of the film. Novels can have the same effect, and sometimes an inner dialogue of pros and cons can accompany the reading, even to the point of withholding final judgment until the end of the book. "Was I wrong to break with my parents' ways? How does this character end up? Then maybe I will know. Will I be proved right or wrong?"

Since the film or novel is a passive adversary or advocate, we can always have the last word; but what is significant is the opening of our awareness to something otherwise obscured or kept at bay. The range of possible reactions is obviously widely variable; some last only as long as the film or novel, others haunt us for months or years. Where we are unwilling to acknowledge the "reality" of something, or where it touches upon something we are not yet able to acknowledge, we may reject the film or novel with a show of emotion that should at least make us aware of our own taboos. Even those films which we take as sheer entertainment can be revelatory. Some of us need happy endings; others find relief in a humorous acceptance of the capriciousness of fate.

There is something therapeutic in coming upon a clear articulation of troublesome and inchoate inner fears and conflicts. It is an old cliché that misery loves company, but to find one is not alone in one's fears and sorrows does alleviate them. An inner miasma can be lifted by clarification and articulation even if they offer no solutions.

Sometimes our identification with an author is so great that we experience a sense of connection with him or her that has nothing to do with time or space. The author may be dead or even unknown, but our appreciation of the depth of common understanding is enough to make us feel that we are not alone in our innermost thoughts and feelings. In that way we find a self-affirmation and self-acceptance that reaches our consciousness through the validation of our positive projection on a symbolic other. Perhaps this is what, in the past, religious projections provided. Erich Neumann, in *Art and the Creative Unconscious*, claims that we have become so one-sided in favor of consciousness, that we have been practically brought to a sclerosis of consciousness that inhibits psychic transformation. This closes us, he says, "both to the *thou* of the Self, of the individual's own wholeness, and to the *thou* of the outside, of the world and mankind." The creative principle, which could unite us in a wholeness of both conscious and unconscious sides of ourselves, no longer has its home, he says, in the symbolism of a cultural canon. It is now living anonymously in the individual. That is why, perhaps, we respond to literature and film which can connect us to our unconscious shadow side through symbolic representations.

This is especially the case when it is a question of the life of the spirit. As previously mentioned, if the cultural canon does not provide us with a collective pattern in which to find meaning in our lives, or spiritual goals to hope for, then we have to create our own patterns as individuals. It is here that the film and novel can play a large part in our lives. What we might be ashamed to acknowledge—because of our cultural bias against the reality of the spirit—we can accept in a film or novel without compromising ourselves. The desire for assurance of life beyond death, of meaning and purpose in life, of goodness valued rather than exploited, of human evolution being part of an underlying purpose in the universe; all these can be acknowledged when we can project our own hidden hopes and desires into that fictional framework. For some, those projections can become a vehicle for soul searching, but short of that, at least it is an avenue for expression. The film *Field of Dreams*, for example, allows us to be playful with those hopes; we can entertain them without having to commit ourselves to anything.

The films and novels that touch us most deeply are the ones we want to share with others, to find out their responses and to see whether they agree with what we have found in them. In comparing our reactions, we often discover new insights or a new depth to our own interpretations. It is with that purpose in mind that I offer these seven chapters, along with the assurance that there is no presumption on my part that these are definitive or exhaustive analyses. My approach is only one perspective, an approach through the analytic psychology of C. G. Jung.

How one approaches a work of art and one's own capacity to see what is there are going to prescribe to some extent what one finds there. Kierkegaard quotes Lichtenberg with a significant aphorism *à propos* of this fact. Referring to Shakespeare's works, Lichtenberg said, "such works are mirrors: when a monkey peers into them, no Apostle can be seen looking out."[7] That warning is enough to cool the ardor of anyone who fancies him- or herself an interpreter of classic works; however, with the renunciation of any claim to producing the final word, a novice can take courage. Good art is infinitely interpretable, and there is room for multiple perspectives. I have chosen the Jungian approach because it is one that opens more doors of interpretation than any other I have encountered. On the other hand, it also offers concrete examples of Jungian concepts that are sometimes only vaguely comprehended or seen only as abstractions. Jung himself referred more than once to literature to give concrete expression to the archetypes he described; for instance, he often referred to Rider Haggard's *She* when he wrote about the anima, and he made many references to Goethe's *Faust* in other contexts.

The answer to "Why literature and film?" can now be seen. It lies with their capacity to reach us on both an abstract intellectual and personal emotional level. In this way they operate much as the Sufi teaching story or the parables of the Bible, which are designed to bring us to self-recognition through our appropriation of them on the affective level. Jung pointed out repeatedly that transformation was impossible without a strong affect accompanying the assimilation of new insights. For the same reasons, literature and film are appropriate in conveying the meaning of individuation as a possible new spiritual path. It is even conceivable that more lives have been changed through the response to literature and film than have been recorded in the analysts' files.

Notes

1. Friedrich Nietzsche, *The Gay Science*, trans. Walter Kaufmann (New York: Random House, Inc., 1974), 181-82.
2. This quotation is taken from a poem by Hölderlin. It is cited by Jung in *Modern Man in Search of a Soul* (Orlando: Harcourt Brace Jovanovich Publishers, 1933), 220.
3. Carl Gustav Jung, *Collected Works* vol. 10, trans. R. F. C. Hull (Princeton: Princeton University Press, 1964), 79.
4. Jung, *Collected Works*, 302-03.
5. Carl Gustav Jung, *On the Nature of the Psyche*, trans. R. F. C. Hull (Princeton: Princeton University Press, 1960), 135-36.
6. R. D. Laing, *The Divided Self* (New York: Penguin Books, 1965), 153-56.
7. Sören Kierkegaard, *Stages of Life's Way* (New York: Schocken Books, 1967), Frontispiece.

PART ONE: INDIVIDUAL PATHS

CHAPTER ONE

Nature's Gift: The Individuation of an Ogre

Zorba the Greek

> So often among so called "primitives" one comes across spiritual personalities who immediately inspire respect, as though they were the fully matured products of an undisturbed fate.[1]
>
> C. G. Jung

In *Report to Greco*, Kazantzakis pays homage to his compatriot Zorba as one of the few people who "left their traces" in his soul. If his description of Zorba in the *Report* is believable, then there is little that is fictional in the character he created in *Zorba the Greek*; the same "larger than life" description appears in both books. In the end, however, it matters little whether Zorba is real, fictional, or remembered only through the film portrayal by Anthony Quinn; Zorba is all of them, an unforgettable and powerful personality who makes us lesser beings both a bit ashamed of our own tepid lives and, at the same time, vicariously proud of the human spirit.

What gives Zorba his power? If we look at his character through Jungian eyes, we see a man who has achieved completeness through courageously allowing and suffering his own unique life to unfold. This process, which Jung called "natural individuation," is, however, in at least one respect "unnatural," since relatively few people ever arrive unaided at that goal.

In *Report to Greco*, Kazantzakis claims that he rarely opened his mouth during the evenings he spent with Zorba eating and drinking on the Cretan shore. It was Zorba who talked, danced, sang, shouted, stamped, and played the Santir. It was Kazantzakis who listened. "What," he writes, "could an 'intellectual' say to an ogre?" And perhaps that is the clue; it may take an ogre to achieve on his own the fruition of a process which Jung describes as both natural and yet too demanding for most people.

There is, in fact, a certain ambiguity in Jung's account of the individuation process as a "law of nature." On the one hand he identifies it as a natural process of growth, akin to the acorn becoming an oak. Yet he also uses the term "natural" when he is distinguishing an unaided process from one in which a person is led, through special techniques, to intensify and deepen consciousness. The ambiguity is only apparent, however, since the same power is at work in all instances and there would be no guided process that would be effective were this not the case. The goal of both "natural" and intentionally aided transformations is the integration and synthesis of the Self.

Three options thus emerge in this process. First: In unconscious individuation the person lacks reflective awareness of the transformative process he is undergoing. Second: He may consciously reflect upon this process and upon the goal toward which he is moving. Third: He may be actively guided into conscious growth and awareness through the assistance of a trained analyst. In *Two Essays on Analytical Psychology*, Jung claims that the natural process of individuation served him as both a model and a guiding principle for his method of treatment.

In *The Way of Individuation*, Jolande Jacobi gives the following account of natural individuation:

> There are people who, entirely by themselves, without using special methods or needing any guidance, let alone the help of analysis, win to that wholeness and wisdom which are the fruit of a life consciously experienced and assimilated, all of its battles fought. . . . The true goal is a task that continues right up to life's evening, namely, the most complete and comprehensive development of the personality. . . . It is not the length of life and not its freedom from disturbances which are the decisive factors in the success of individuation but, as we have seen, the draining of life to the full, in the good and the difficult alike.[2]

What is essential is the courage with which one involves oneself in life, without trying to escape the risks that life sets before one. The person who is capable of natural transformation will not fear life's struggles but will enter into them, living out all the experiences that come one's way. Only then will the maturing and fulfillment of one's being emerge. It cannot happen to those whose fear for safety and security leads them to sidestep their struggles or to hide themselves from the risks. All human beings, then, have the capacity for health and wholeness, and a natural goal of differentiating, integrating, and developing their own personalities.

The special methods of the guided process belong to the therapeutic disciplines, and much has been written on this subject in the form of case histories in both professional and popular literature. On the other hand, those who approach individuation through their own efforts do not usually appear in analysts' offices nor, consequently, in their literature. They can be found, however, in fiction. Zorba, in Kazantzakis' *Zorba the Greek*, is an extraordinary character who can be interpreted in that light.

In Jungian terms, progression toward wholeness begins with the development and adaptation to the world through one's dominant function, which also determines one's psychological type. On the basis of the paired opposites—thinking/feeling and sensation/intuition, one function will gain precedence in the conscious personality, and along with the adopted attitude—extraversion or introversion—will govern the typical conscious development of that person.

With our first introduction to them, Zorba and the boss are revealed as opposite types or shadow figures of each other. Zorba is the extraverted feeling/sensation complement to the boss's thinking/intuiting introversion. Opposite types are attracted to each other, since each represents what is lacking in the other. That attraction is obvious when, in the opening chapter of the book, Zorba bursts upon the meditative withdrawal of the boss, first with his intense stare through the glass door and then his rapid approach, greeting the boss with "Traveling? Taking me with you?" Upon the boss's query of "Why?" Zorba responds with a shrug and a characteristic assertion. "Why! Why! Can't a man do anything without a why? Just like that, because he wants to?"

Again and again the boss is shaken out of his self-absorption by the explosions of Zorba's wonder with the world. Zorba's immediacy brings a new sense of value to the boss.

> Things we are accustomed to, and which we pass by indifferently, suddenly rise up in front of Zorba like fearful enigmas. Seeing a woman pass by, he stops in consternation. "What is that mystery?" he asks. "What is a woman, and why does she turn our heads? Just tell me, I ask you, what's the meaning of that?"
>
> He interrogates himself with the same amazement when he sees a man, a tree in blossom, a glass of cold water. Zorba sees everything every day as if for

the first time. . . . I felt, as I listened to Zorba, that the world was recovering its pristine freshness. All the dulled daily things regained the brightness they had in the beginning, when we came out of the hands of God. Water, women, the stars, bread, returned to their mysterious primitive origin and the divine whirlwind burst once more upon the air.[3]

Von Franz describes the extraverted feeling type as one who makes friends easily, has few illusions about people, and makes appropriate evaluations of their positive and negative sides.

> These are well adjusted, very reasonable people who roll along amiably through society, can get what they want quite easily, and can somehow arrange it that everybody is willing to give them what they want. They lubricate their surroundings so marvelously that life goes along very easily.[4]

Zorba is all that, but he is equally at home in the world of inanimate objects. The boss describes him at work:

> He could feel the ramifications of the galleries like veins in his flesh, and what the dark masses of coal could not feel, Zorba felt with a conscious human lucidity. . . . He was completely absorbed in his tasks: he thought of nothing else; he was one with the earth, the pick and the coal. He and the hammer and nails were united in the struggle with the wood.[5]

Where feeling is the dominant function, thinking is the inferior function and will, therefore, be the least developed of the functions. Zorba proves no exception to this rule. From the beginning, we are aware of Zorba's distrust of human reason. "The backside of the miller's wife, that's human reason."[6] His contempt for logic is revealed through the two theories he offers to share with the old bishop at the monastery. The first theory is "two and two make four"; the second theory is "two and two do not make four." When the old man stammers that he doesn't understand, Zorba says "Neither do I!"[7] and bursts into laughter.

He insists more than once that his brain is "not the correct weight" and warns the boss about trusting him when he conceives the idea of the cable railway. The idea for the cable system hits Zorba with all the numinosity of a spiritual revelation. He becomes obsessed with the idea, making models, drawing pictures, and roaming the mountain looking for just the right place to set it up. According to von Franz, if an extraverted feeling type once starts to think, he becomes completely caught up in it. She also claims that this type dislikes most of all introverted thinking, thinking involving philosophical principles or abstractions. Characteristically, Zorba is uncomfortable with the abstract thinking of the boss. He understands ideas best when they are expressed symbolically, through dancing, music, or through stories.

> When we reached the hut, he sat on crossed legs, placed the *santuri* on his knees and lowered his head, lost in deep meditation. It was as if he were listening, with his head on his chest, to innumerable songs and trying to choose one, the most beautiful and most despairing of all. He at last made his choice and started a heart-rending air. From time to time he eyed me slant wise. I felt that what he could not or dare not tell me in words he was saying with the *santuri*. That I was wasting my life, that the widow and I were two insects who live but a second beneath the sun, then die for all eternity. Never more! Never more![8]

Zorba often draws pictures. He draws a picture of Bouboulina as a mermaid, with her four admirals, one in each corner; he also draws a picture of the cable railway, with a monk in each of the four corners. On listening to the boss explain that life is the struggle to turn matter into spirit, Zorba scratches his head and claims a thick skull. "Ah, if only you could dance all that you've just said, then I'd understand."[9] Or, he argues, if only he could tell it in a story, like the one the old Turk told him—"that neither the seven stories of heaven nor the seven stories of the earth are enough to contain God; but a man's heart can contain him. So be very careful . . . never to wound a man's heart!"[10] The boss, Zorba points out, understands with his brain, but while he talks his arms and chest are silent. "Well, what do you think you understand with? With your head? Bah!"[11]

Zorba has contempt for those who write about life instead of living it. When the boss sneers, "Why don't you write a book yourself and explain all the mysteries of the world to us?"[12] Zorba answers:

> Why not? For the simple reason that I live all those mysteries as you call them, and I haven't the time to write. Sometimes it's war, sometimes women, sometimes wine, sometimes the *santuri*; where would I find time to drive a miserable pen? That's how the business falls into the hands of the pen pushers! . . . all those who have the time don't live them! D'you see?[13]

Zorba is not intimidated by the superior intellect of the boss. When it comes to dealing with reality, he tells the boss, "I don't think your brain is quite formed yet."[14] He also criticizes the boss for his faint-heartedness in accepting life with all its trouble. "Life is trouble!"[15] asserts Zorba.

According to Jung, it is through the inferior function that we are most vulnerable to intrusions by our unconscious shadow side. Confrontation with the shadow is a painful process, because it forces us to become conscious and to make difficult moral choices. Zorba does not escape that painful confrontation. He tells the boss of two events in his life which changed him. The first is Zorba's account of himself as a callow youth who was cruelly destructive in his remarks to his eighty-year-old grandmother, ridiculing her for pretending that the young men serenading a neighboring young woman were serenading her. In the face of his jeering scorn of her, the old grandmother goes into an immediate decline. When she dies two months later, she curses him, wishing him the same fate. Zorba admits that her curse hit home. "I am in my sixty-fifth year, I think, but even if I live to be a hundred I'll never lay off. I'll still have a little mirror in my pocket, and I'll still be running after the female of the species.[16] Zorba is reminded of this story when he reproaches the boss for letting Bouboulina see them laughing at her.

Another painful encounter with his shadow occurred during the years of his fighting for Greece against the Turks and the Bulgars. Zorba fought with passion and courage, never questioning his acts of violence—until the day he encountered five children begging in the street, and learned that they had been orphaned by him, that it was he who had killed their father. That moment of truth ended his participation in the war. He tells the boss, "that was how I was rescued."

> Rescued from my country, from priests, and from money. I began sifting things, sifting more and more things out. I lighten my burden that way I—how shall I put it?—I find my own deliverance, I become a man. . . . There was a time when I used to say: that man's a Turk, or a Bulgar, or a Greek. I've done things for my country that would make your hair stand on end, boss. I've cut people's throats, burned villages, robbed and raped women, wiped out entire families. Why? Because they were Bulgars, or Turks. "Bah! to hell with you you swine!" I say to myself sometimes "To hell with you right away, you ass." Nowadays I say this man is a good fellow, that one's a bastard. They can be Greeks or Bulgars or Turks, it doesn't matter. Is he good? Or is he bad? That's the only thing I ask nowadays. And as I grow older—I'd swear this on the last crust I eat—I feel I shan't even go on asking that! Whether a man's good or bad, I'm sorry for him, for all of 'em. The sight of a man just rends my insides, even if I act as though I don't care a damn! There he is, poor devil, I think; he also eats and drinks and makes love and is frightened, whoever he is: he has his God and his devil just the same, and he'll peg out and lie as stiff as a board beneath the ground and be food for worms, just the same. Poor devil! We're all brothers! All worm meat![17]

One aspect of Zorba's character deserves special attention because it could raise doubts about his individuation, namely, his often degrading and patronizing descriptions of women. How developed can a man be who persists in describing women as "poor creatures, sickly and fretful," wanting nothing in life beyond caresses from a man? To make matters worse, Zorba seems to find women interchangeable. They are "the female of the species," a generic title that seems to deny them any individuality at all. Is Zorba merely showing us the provincial Greek of his time? Perhaps, but there may be a better way to interpret his behavior.

Zorba has a highly developed feeling function. He is able to differentiate and adapt to situations with men and women alike and to smooth the way in numerous potentially explosive situations. For example, he manages, with tact and kindness, the engagement ceremony on the beach, accepting the dishonest situation in which the boss has put him through the bogus marriage proposal and turning it from a mockery into a celebration of human dignity. Also worth noting is the protective and tender care he shows Bouboulina when she is dying, and his return to her room after it has been stripped of all her belongings by the invasion of the townspeople who remove everything except the parrot. Zorba takes on the care of the parrot as a mark of loyalty to Bouboulina and says a reverent goodbye to the poor little foreigner.

Again, when Manolakas challenges him for having disgraced him by overpowering him in the struggle for the widow's life, Zorba tries to save the younger man's pride. "I didn't disgrace you, Manolakas! Beat it, I say. You're a big, strong fellow, yes, but luck was against you . . . and luck is blind, didn't you know that?"[18] When the boss succeeds in talking them into shaking hands, Zorba says, "You've got a strong grip, Manolakas. . . . You're a stout fellow and pretty tough!"[19]

With such a capacity to feel for the dignity of others, how can Zorba call women "pitiful creatures" and "the female of the species?" This seeming inconsistency may be explained if we recognize that a conscious integration of the feminine in Zorba is nowhere near the level of his differentiated feeling. The possibility of such a discrepancy also makes a good argument for not identifying the feminine principle (Eros) with the feeling function.

Von Franz, in her chapter on "Individuation" in *Man and His Symbols*, points out the tendency on the part of young men, who are still at a primitive stage of anima development, to be non-differentiating in their choice of love object. In one respect, Zorba, in his appreciation for the "female of the species" pays women a great compliment; but, in that their value for him has no personal or individual focus, the appreciation has a somewhat hollow ring. On the other hand, he is a very present and attentive lover and prides himself on the fact that he forgets everything else when he is with a woman.

If the paradox of Zorba's attitude to women is understood, however, as a function of the discrepancy between an immature level of anima integration along with a fine discrimination of feeling and sensation, then one also understands the compassion and sensitivity in his behavior with women in spite of the collective and derogatory way in which he describes them.

While the above explanation may account for Zorba's ambiguous relation to women, it raises yet another question. To what extent can a man be considered as well on the path to individuation if he is still responding to women as a non-differentiating adolescent? The answer to that question may be found in Jung's assertion that psychic wholeness is not synonymous with perfection. "There is no light without shadow and no psychic wholeness without imperfection. To round itself out, life calls not for perfection but for completeness; and for this the 'thorn in the flesh' is needed, the suffering of defects without which there is no progress and no ascent."[20]

Since suffering through all one's defects is a life-long process, so is the process of transformation. In his last letter, Zorba reveals that he is respectably married and about to become a father. Wearing poor Bouboulina's treasured wedding ring, he does not neglect to acknowledge that gift; "God bless her remains!"

In contrast to Zorba, the boss resists a natural process of transformation.

> Whether one goes the "natural," more or less unconscious way of individuation or takes the consciously worked through way depends, presumably, on fate. But one thing is certain: unconsciousness or wanting to remain unconscious, to escape the call to development and avoid the venture of life, is sin. For though growing old is the inescapable lot of all creatures, growing old meaningfully is a task ordained for man alone. What meaning has our life? None but what *we* give it.[21]

The boss, an intellectual and a "pen pusher," is caught in an obsessive asceticism, which is both a function of his inhibitions as a thinking type and his commitment to Buddhist ideology. Aboard ship on the way to Crete, he looks at the world from what he describes as a Buddhist compassion "as cold as the conclusion of a metaphysical syllogism. A compassion not only for men but for all life which struggles, cries, weeps, hopes and does not perceive that everything is a phantasmagoria of nothingness."[22] He longs for the day when he can retire into solitude, without joy or sorrow and with only the knowledge that all living is a dream. That possibility he sees as a promise of freedom. When life does threaten to involve him in its joys and sorrows, he escapes in his books. Despising the pleasures of the flesh, even eating can seem to him a shameful act. But Zorba will have none of his asceticism and insists that the body, too, has a soul and needs to eat. "Everything in good time. In front of us now is the pilaff; let our minds become pilaff."[23]

To the boss's eyes the hidden meaning of the world is found in the illusion of its reality; and in this melancholy mood, he is stung by the contrast of his own alienation with Zorba's joyful and vital presence. He resolves to escape from Buddha, to rid himself of all his metaphysical care and anxiety. How? By a resolution to make direct and firm contact with men.

But his resolution is easier made than put into effect and his obsession with Buddhist beliefs does not fade away with his decision to abandon them. It is only the urgent creative voice within him which shows him the way to free himself; he will write a life of Buddha.

When his inner obsession with Buddha gains outer expression on paper, a slow transformation begins.

> My life is wasted, I thought. If only I could take a cloth and wipe out all I have learnt, all I have seen and heard, and go to Zorba's school and start the great, the real alphabet! What a different road I would choose. I should keep my five senses perfectly trained, and my whole body, too, so that it would enjoy and understand. . . . I should fill my soul with flesh. I should fill my flesh with soul. In fact, I should reconcile at last within me the two eternal antagonists.[24]

As the transformation occurs, even his escape into literature loses its power; he realizes his former enchantment as cerebral acrobatics and has a sudden revelation that Buddha is the Last Man. With that realization comes a new freedom; for the Last Man also means a new beginning.

A conversion from one extreme to its opposite is what Jung called the process of enantiodromia. The boss, in his desire to exchange Buddha for Zorba does not quite achieve that conversion; but he does make a new beginning in that direction. What he is not able to do, however, is to alter his orientation as thinker and thereby alter his inferior feeling. For example, when he responds with pity for Bouboulina who is desperate in her need to hear that Zorba has not forgotten her, the boss, unadapted in the nuances of feeling, goes too far and "reads" a marriage proposal into Zorba's letter. No one sensitive to the feelings of others would dare to pull such a trick; for it would be a very cruel joke to play on Bouboulina had Zorba refused to take responsibility for the boss's deception and told her the truth. As for Zorba, that insensitive joke put him in the precarious position of a moral dilemma, damned if he does and damned if he doesn't. Only because Zorba was big enough in spirit and resourceful enough to carry off the outdoor engagement ceremony, was everyone spared a painful outcome.

In his own romantic exploits with the widow, the boss is equally inept. His immediate reaction to her is that of a neurotic ascetic; he projects Mara, the Spirit of the Evil One in the shape of a woman, on her. Obsessed as he is with the desire of transforming matter into spirit, he persists in subduing his desires, at the same time bitterly condemning himself for the sin of refusing to honor both the woman and his own desire. When his body finally leads him to hover at her gate, he is still thinking of her as a "wild beast . . . fat and voracious . . . like some female insects who devour the males."[25] Although he gives in and spends the night with the widow, his reflections the following day are totally self-preoccupied. He reflects upon his body, his soul, his growth, with no mention of the widow at all. This preoccupation with his own reactions is typical of an introvert; but if the experience were a transformative one, some reference to his feeling for the widow would be expected. On the contrary, the desired and dreaded union appears to have only a therapeutic meaning for him.

> My body was light and contented, like an animal after the hunt, when it has caught and eaten its prey and is lying in the sun, licking its lips. My mind, a body too in its way, was resting contented. It seemed to have found a marvelously simple answer to the vital complicated problems which tormented it.
>
> All of the joy of the previous night flowed back from the innermost depths of my being, spread out into fresh courses and abundantly watered the earth of which I was made. As I lay, with my eyes closed, I seemed to hear my being bursting its shell and growing larger. That night, for the first time, I felt clearly that the soul is flesh as well, perhaps more volatile, more diaphanous, perhaps freer, but flesh all the same.[26]

The death of the widow has even less power to draw him fully into life. He compares his withdrawal into abstraction to the response of Zorba, a "real Man" who is able to suffer, to feel sorrow, and who doesn't spoil his sorrow or joy by "running it through the fine sieve of metaphysics." The boss, in contrast and to his despair, in his "wretched, inhuman way" proceeds to transpose reality and to reduce it to the abstract, intellectualizing the widow's death until he arrives at the awful conclusion that what had happened was necessary and contributed to the universal harmony. The widow becomes a symbol, at rest in his memory. "The terrible events of that one day broadened, extended into time and space, and became one with great past civilizations; the civilizations became one with the earth's destiny; the earth with the destiny of the universe—and thus, returning to the widow, I found her subject to the great laws of existence, reconciled with her murderers, immobile and serene."[27]

In this way the boss dispenses with the threat of panic and suffering. He is not ready to allow himself to feel the loss of the widow or the fear of death. He transmutes it all into abstract thought.

For the boss, the goal of individuation seems a long way off. In spite of his deliverance from asceticism, and even his learning to dance, the boss remains very much the intellectual, cautious and disciplined, distrustful of committed action, a detached spectator of his own life. Although his new philosophy celebrates engagement instead of asceticism, a change which marks some expansion of the spirit, he is still "falling into words." The new words suggest a creative evolution in which we play our part in the service of something immortal; yet at bottom this is but another version of his asceticism, another formula for transforming matter into spirit. ". . . everything, men, animals, trees, stars, we are all one, we are all one substance involved in the same terrible struggle. What struggle? . . . Turning matter into spirit."[28]

Zorba rejoices over the new awakening in the boss and teaches him to dance. But he also sees what is missing in the boss, who is limited by the little shopkeeper who keeps accounts in his head. He tells him that he lacks one important thing; he has no madness. Zorba wants him to forget the accounts, to open himself to spontaneity, even to recklessness. Years later, Zorba makes one last attempt to bring forth that missing madness when he invites the boss to come and see a wonderful green stone. The wonderful green stone is rich in symbolic meaning. The stone is a symbol of wholeness; it is one with the jewel or pearl of great price, the ruby, the philosophers' stone—all symbolic of the completed or individuated soul. Zorba has found it; but the boss does not see Zorba's stone, nor does he find his own.

Zorba, well on the path to completion, has arrived at the expression of his own unique personality through the arduous process of consciously living through and honestly facing the challenge of the joys, sorrows, and passions that life has opened out to him. His convictions are far from conventional, but he arrived at them from the ground of his own experience and he is not troubled by the discrepancy between his beliefs and the opinions of the world. He has learned to trust in himself, and his independence of spirit and affirmation of life are rooted in that experience.

The boss, whose body and mind are still at war with one another, admires and envies the way in which, for Zorba, body and mind form one harmonious whole. "I had never seen such a friendly accord between a man and the universe."[29] The friendly accord comes not from any metaphysical assurance or mystic connection, however, but from his own self-acceptance and his openness to the world around him. Zorba insists that the devil and God are the same, but, in fact, he believes in neither. His identification of them is his own way of denying the traditional separation of an Absolute Good and Evil and his own way of asserting that the universe is amoral and, to man, a mystery.

"If I believed in man, I'd believe in God, and I'd believe in the devil, too."
... "Don't you believe in anything?" the boss asks. Zorba answers: "No,
... I don't believe in anything or anyone; only in Zorba... because he's the
only being I have in my power, the only one I know.... When I die,
everything'll die. The whole Zorbatic world will go to the bottom!"[30]

Zorba is convinced that God-or-the-devil won't bother himself about what Zorba eats, what he does, what commandments he breaks. And since God and the devil are the same, it doesn't matter which one finally "carries him off."

He learned through his own experience how to free himself from passions and obsessions, not by turning ascetic, but by the opposite means, stuffing oneself until one bursts, and he arrives at his own viewpoint on how to live an authentic life: "I carry on as if I was going to die any minute."[31] The latter was Zorba's answer to the old man who told him that *he* carried on as if he would never die. Zorba keeps the inevitability of his death as a live option before his consciousness so that his responsibility for and joy in the present and its uniqueness as *his* will not escape his awareness. He does not deny the suffering in life, but he refuses to be defeated by suffering. "Every time I suffer, boss . . . it just cracks my heart in two. But it's all scarred and riddled with wounds already, and it sticks itself together again in a trice and the wound can't be seen. I'm covered with healed wounds, that's why I can stand so much."[32]

In *Jung's Typology*, von Franz describes the situation of one who reaches the point of integrating the four functions, where some middle ground is reached. At this point, the ego and its conscious activity are no longer identified with or under the dominance of a particular function. When asked what that person would look like, von Franz answered that the nearest example would be similar to the behavior of Zen Buddhist Masters.

> He continues in everyday life, participating in it in a normal way. If people come to be taught, he will teach them with feeling. If a difficult problem is put before him, he can think about it. If it is the moment to eat, he will eat, and if it is the moment to sleep, he will sleep; he uses his sensation function in the right way. When it is a question of seeing through the other person in a flash of intuition, or through the situation, he will do that. He will not, however, be inwardly bound to the ego functions he uses in meeting the particular situation.[33]

(Von Franz's interpretation of a Buddhist Master offers a striking contrast to the highly ascetic interpretation of Buddhism by the boss. Whatever

Kazantzakis' own interpretation may have been, in *Report to Greco* he cites Buddha as one of the most profound influences in his life.)

Zorba is not a Zen Master, but, when he tries to explain himself to the boss, he describes a mode of consciousness that approaches von Franz's description.

> I've stopped thinking all the time of what happened yesterday. And stopped asking myself what's going to happen tomorrow. What's happening today, this minute, that's what I care about. I say: "What are you doing at this moment, Zorba?" "I'm sleeping." "Well, sleep well." "What are you doing at this moment, Zorba?" "I'm working." "Well, work well." "What are you doing at this moment, Zorba?" "I'm kissing a woman." "Well, kiss her well, Zorba! And forget all the rest while you're doing it; there's nothing else on earth, only you and her! Get on with it!"[34]

In one important way, Zorba is far from a Zen Master; he lives with unanswered questions that surface with his anguish over death and suffering. He holds God responsible for a defective creation, even blaming Him for the fact that Bouboulina falls asleep at the New Year's dinner. "It is all the fault," he says, "of that Grand Hare-brained Harum-Scarum, the Grand Suleiman Pasha.... You know who!"[35]

When Zorba describes his former violence, and all the violence that led finally to the liberation of Crete, he expresses his bewilderment with a God who rewards such violence. "Instead of wiping us out with a thunderbolt, God gives us liberty! I just don't understand."[36] Why, he wonders, should rewards not come from kindness and honesty? But he does not dwell for long upon such questions. When Zorba cannot find an answer, he brushes the question aside with a characteristic assertion that the world is a mystery and man is just a great brute. Some questions, however, obstinately recur. Living with the idea of death does not reconcile him to it, nor does anything justify it in Zorba's eyes. He asks the boss why people die, expecting an answer from all the boss's books. But the boss, at a loss for the answer, responds with a parable aimed at conveying affirmation of our human finitude. Zorba refuses to make such an affirmation. After reflection on the idea, he says: "You know ... I think of death every second. I look at it and I'm not frightened. But never, never, do I say I like it. No, I don't like it at all! I don't agree!"[37]

His outrage at the boss's advocacy of affirmation echoes his former response to the widow's death.

> I tell you, boss, everything that happens in this world is unjust, unjust, unjust! I won't be a party to it! I, Zorba, the worm, the slug! Why must the

young die and the old wrecks go on living? Why do little children die? I had a boy once—Dmitri he was called—and I lost him when he was three years old. Well . . . I shall never, never forgive God for that, do you hear? I tell you, the day I die, if He has the cheek to appear in front of me, and if He is really and truly a God, He'll be ashamed! Yes, yes, He'll be ashamed to show himself to Zorba, the slug![38]

In *The Brothers Karamazov*, Ivan, who also calls himself a worm, makes a similar accusation of injustice and refuses God's world; yet he nevertheless suffers from unconscious moral guilt. Zorba, on the contrary, has no pangs of conscience over his rebellion against God and God's moral order. Nor does he torture himself over the unanswered questions which remain. When it becomes clear that the boss can offer no answers for him, Zorba returns to the concreteness of life. "Good night, boss. That's enough."

His return carries no bitterness. If life is a mystery, it is still to be lived to the fullest. Only old age holds terror for Zorba. Old age he sees as a disgrace, and he confesses in a letter to the boss that he is ashamed of it, even if only before himself. The struggle against that indignity lasts until his last breath, when he pulls himself over to the window to look at the mountains and to laugh one more time. His refusal of a priest and his objection to the injustice of death remain along with his acceptance of its inevitability. Zorba lives his own death, as he lived his own life. His last words are: "I've done heaps and heaps of things in my life, but I still did not do enough. Men like me ought to live a thousand years. Good night!"[39]

Notes

1. Carl Gustav Jung, *Psychological Reflections*, eds. Jolande Jacobi and R. F. C. Hull (Princeton: Princeton University Press, 1974), 314.
2. Jolande Jacobi, *The Way of Individuation* (New York: Meridian Book, New American Library, 1983), 17-18.
3. Nikos Kazantzakis, *Zorba the Greek* (New York: Simon & Schuster, 1952), 51.
4. Marie-Louise von Franz, *Jung's Typology* (New York: Spring Publications, 1971), 43.
5. Kazantzakis, *Zorba*, 108-9.
6. Kazantzakis, *Zorba*, 11.
7. Kazantzakis, *Zorba*, 205.
8. Kazantzakis, *Zorba*, 102.
9. Kazantzakis, *Zorba*, 278.
10. Kazantzakis, *Zorba*, 278.
11. Kazantzakis, *Zorba*, 223.
12. Kazantzakis, *Zorba*, 217.
13. Kazantzakis, *Zorba*, 217.

14. Kazantzakis, *Zorba*, 53. He also accuses the boss of having a shopkeeper's brain (p. 10, p. 300).
15. Kazantzakis, *Zorba*, 101.
16. Kazantzakis, *Zorba*, 47.
17. Kazantzakis, *Zorba*, 225-26.
18. Kazantzakis, *Zorba*, 251.
19. Kazantzakis, *Zorba*, 252.
20. Jung, *Psychological Reflections*, 315.
21. Jacobi, *The Way of Individuation*, 131.
22. Kazantzakis, *Zorba*, 17.
23. Kazantzakis, *Zorba*, 35.
24. Kazantzakis, *Zorba*, 74.
25. Kazantzakis, *Zorba*, 236.
26. Kazantzakis, *Zorba*, 237.
27. Kazantzakis, *Zorba*, 249.
28. Kazantzakis, *Zorba*, 278.
29. Kazantzakis, *Zorba*, 132.
30. Kazantzakis, *Zorba*, 54.
31. Kazantzakis, *Zorba*, 35.
32. Kazantzakis, *Zorba*, 272.
33. Von Franz, *Jung's Typology*, 64.
34. Kazantzakis, *Zorba*, 273.
35. Kazantzakis, *Zorba*, 130-31.
36. Kazantzakis, *Zorba*, 23.
37. Kazantzakis, *Zorba*, 270.
38. Kazantzakis, *Zorba*, 247.
39. Kazantzakis, *Zorba*, 310.

CHAPTER TWO

An Anima Run Amok

The House of the Spirits

> A man needs to be hostile to woman in order to free himself from the "Baubo" that he sees in his mother.... The seed of the anima is only productive when man can subordinate his libido to the female principle. If he does not succeed the anima runs away and the man turns to violence to find himself—to the tormenting of those around him or the boasting of self-importance.[1]
>
> Margaret Ostrowski-Sachs

The House of the Spirits is a novel that can be approached from many directions. Because the dominant male character, Esteban Trueba, is both a narrator and a significant presence throughout three generations of his family's history, an analysis of his development is at the same time a perspective on the novel as a whole.

Trueba is a complex character whose tragic flaw is an ungovernable and explosive temper, which has painful and inescapable consequences for everyone with whom he is intimately connected. While one might be tempted to explain Trueba's character as a product of his time and place in history, one can also interpret it as the expression of a man whose aggressive and one-sided masculinity has limited his development and potentiality for spiritual growth.

If we accept Jung's premise that everyone has a contrasexual aspect to his character that is unconscious and needs to be consciously experienced in order to achieve wholeness or completeness of his being, then Trueba can be seen as a man who is continually limited by his entrapment in repressions and projections.

His own worst enemy, Trueba victimizes himself along with every explosive reaction with which he victimizes those about him. Just as he is unable to take the attempts at self-determination of others seriously when they act contrary to his will, so he ignores his own inner voice, in favor of the narrower will of his conscious personality.

Von Franz describes the way in which the anima, the contrasexual complement to male consciousness, can aid a man in opening his consciousness to inner knowledge.

> Whenever a man's logical mind is incapable of discerning facts that are hidden in his unconscious, the anima helps him to dig them out. Even more vital is the role that the anima plays in putting a man's mind in tune with the right inner values and thereby opening the way into more profound inner depths. It is as if an inner "radio" becomes tuned to a certain wave length that excludes irrelevancies but allows the voice of the Great Man to be heard. In establishing this inner "radio" reception, the anima takes on the role of guide, or mediator, to the world within and to the Self.[2]

Trueba's insistent affirmation of his conscious will is a consistent barrier to any unconscious influence that might open him to his own inner depths. The effects of this barrier can be seen in his personal and social relations as the story unfolds and as the consequences of his actions are revealed. His path toward eventual self-knowledge, which comes only at the end of his long life, traverses the paths of four women, all of whom love him and play a part in his belated transformation. The first is Rosa the Beautiful.

Prior to his meeting with Rosa the Beautiful, Trueba was a more or less serious and self-reliant young man, having to contend with growing up in an unhealthy atmosphere of moral, physical, and spiritual invalidism. His hypertrophied pride may be viewed as a reaction to that childhood—a drunken, irresponsible father who left his wife and children in poverty, an invalid mother, and a martyr sister. Even though humiliation was a daily fare, Trueba was not one to embrace or wallow in it. His refusal to be an accomplice to his sister's martyrdom was an early exercise in the ruthlessness which was to play so great a part in his character. Although Trueba's character is aggressively masculine, his tendency to violence cannot be attributed to anima repression alone, since he is described as having been subject to fits of extreme anger from early childhood.

Physically, Trueba is presented as a handsome, graceful, and powerful man who, despite his frequently sour expression, had an agreeable face with "astonishingly sweet and bright eyes."

Neither the religious fanaticism of his sister nor the remoteness of his mother, with whom he never really felt at ease or really loved, provide a favorable prognosis for love and marriage. Trueba's contempt for women had an early start. But conscious contempt often covers unconscious idealization. From the moment Trueba sees Rosa, he succumbs to a classic infatuation. According to Jung, such love at first sight is always an anima projection. Trueba's captivation, however, is hardly unique to him, for Rosa is a young woman whose mere appearance constellates collective infatuations and projections. Crowds of men peer at her, awe-struck, wherever she goes. With her other-worldly beauty, green hair, yellow eyes, and white, smooth, porcelain skin, she is more mermaid or water sprite than woman. Dreamy and detached, she has a way of moving that is more like flying; she is like an apparition.

Trueba, seeing her for the first time, is dumbstruck and follows her as though hypnotized. With his fierce pride and will, he decides she is the only woman for him and dares to become her official suitor, a task which frightened away lesser men. With his new love, Trueba finds a goal in life—to become rich and, therefore, worthy of Rosa.

Rosa's accidental and untimely death temporarily destroys all meaning in life for Trueba and brings out his colossal rage, as he pounds the walls, rips up her letters and drawings, and insists, against the rules, on remaining all night in the graveyard.

Before Rosa, Trueba never thought of love, and romance struck him as dangerous and pointless. He was also afraid of being rejected. But the experience of being in love, even though aborted, changed something in Trueba. He now knew two things: that he was not rejected and that he had lost something valuable. Something was now missing from his life that he was not aware of missing before he knew Rosa. He also found a goal in life—to become rich and powerful. In this way some measure of change and self-knowledge was acquired. Since the projection on Rosa was more collective than personal, the insight he acquired could not be called transformative, but it did open him to new possibilities.

On the neglected country estate of his family, Trueba found temporary salvation by throwing himself into the hard physical labor of restoring the land and turning it once more into a productive property. He also found solace in a harsh and predatory sexuality with the young peasant girls of his estate, a far different sexuality than he had imagined with Rosa.

Trueba separates the women of his social class from those of the peasant class, whom he treats indiscriminately as objects to be used and discarded at his pleasure. Neither in one nor the other class, however, does he recognize the individual woman—with the possible exception of the determined young prostitute, Transito Soto, to whom he lends money so that she can pursue her goal of a successful career in the Capitol.

Trueba's paternalism toward his peasants parallels his attitude toward women. Patriarchal toward both, he fails to recognize any reciprocity in human dignity or self-determination between himself and the peasants or between himself and the women he encounters. He disparages both peasants and women as child-like, needing the governance and decisions which he bestows as his privilege and responsibility. Speaking of the peasants: "These poor people are completely ignorant and uneducated. They're like children, they can't handle responsibility. How could *they* know what's best for them? Without me they'd be lost . . ."[3] In regard to Clara's mother, Nivea, who campaigned for women's rights, he says: "That woman is sick in the head! . . . It would go against nature. If women don't know that two and two are four, how are they going to be able to handle a scalpel? Their duty is motherhood and the home . . . What these cases really need is a strong hand."[4]

He prides himself on the superior qualities of those of his sex and class without ever recognizing the contradictions in their behavior. For instance, Trueba announces to his club members after the election:

> This country's a genuine republic. We have civic pride. Here the Conservative Party wins cleanly and openly, and we don't need a general to keep things orderly and calm, not like the neighboring dictatorships where they kill each other off while the gringos walk away with all their raw materials.[5]

What Trueba leaves out in his speech is that the *patróns* used their usual tactics to make sure that the peasants voted in their favor, tactics which utilized the persuasive effects of wine, meat, song, and phony fellowship. As reinforcement, should all that good will prove insufficient, the peasants were warned that they would lose their jobs if they failed to vote conservative, and as back up, the officials were also bribed.

Self-satisfied, Trueba experiences no conflict between word and action in his assertion of politial purity. His will to find himself honorable is an effective barrier against any threat, whether from private or public life, which would raise any self-doubts. That he idealizes women of his own class, while raping and discarding peasant girls at his pleasure, presents no problems in logic or ethics for him. If the anima of Trueba is working toward provoking any self-confrontation, at this point she is fighting a losing battle. No self-doubts are allowed conscious expression.

Trueba even refuses to acknowledge any bastard sons, of which there were many, other than the one of Pancha, the first peasant girl he rapes, and even that child he gives no special consideration and soon forgets. In his material goals, however, he is successful; the estate is flourishing, the peasants have a better life, and he has become rich and respected in the community.

The death of Trueba's mother brings him back to the Capitol and to the second and most important woman in his life, Rosa's young sister Clara, the clairvoyant.

Trueba's marriage with Clara is not only what Jung has called a medieval marriage—the wife living out the husband's femininity and the husband living out the wife's masculinity—but Trueba and Clara are opposites in all ways. Clara retreats into spiritual life, in contrast to Trueba's materiality and pragmatism. Her behavior is unconventional while he demands social conformity. She is spontaneous and original while he is rigidly conservative. She has an unshakable equanimity, even in response to his terrifying rages. They are two foreign countries, neither speaking the other's language; however, one difference is crucial. Trueba is maddened by his inability to penetrate Clara's self-containment. In her spiritual detachment from him, she is inaccessible to his driving will for dominance. Oblivious to his raging tirades, she is simply uninterested in his need to dominate her.

For example, when Trueba discovers that Clara has been introducing her mother's women's rights slogans to the peasant women whom she has been teaching to sew and to treat common diseases, she has her first experience of his famous tantrums.

> He shouted like a madman, pacing up and down the living room and slamming his fist against the furniture, arguing that if Clara intended to follow in her mother's footsteps she was going to come face to face with a real man, who would pull her pants down and give her a good spanking so she'd get it out of her damned head to go around haranguing people, and that he categorically forbade her to go to prayer meetings or any other kind and that he wasn't some ninny whose wife could go around making a fool of him. Clara let him scream his head off and bang on the furniture until he was exhausted. Then, inattentive as ever, she asked him if he knew how to wiggle his ears.[6]

Nothing Trueba does has influence on Clara. His obsessive love demanded complete dependence; he wanted her to have no life outside of him. But the reality was that "the woman sleeping by his side was not really there; she was in some unknown, other dimension where he could never reach."[7]

His relation with Clara is the outer expression of Trueba's failure to relate to his own contrasexual femininity, both being inaccessible, unreachable, unconnected to him. Both failures are due to his own willful insistence that any connection be on his own terms, terms demanding complete submission to his conscious domination. But the inner soul cannot be willed into conscious submission to the ego, and any attempt to do so only leads to suffering and frustration. So it happens to Trueba. He loses both Clara and access to his own inner being and is left with his rage and his damaged spirit. His willful determination to conquer Clara on those terms suggests that he is in an inflated state, caught up in his identification with a collective patriarchal consciousness. When the inevitable downfall occurs, he interprets it in terms of his sister Ferula's curse. Ferula warned him that he would shrink in body and soul and die alone. Always the materialist, Trueba experiences the inevitable deflation of his ego as a physical shrinking of his body. Although no one but Trueba notices that he is shrinking, he is convinced that Ferula's curse has taken effect. Thus Trueba does not escape the effects of an intrusion from the unconscious, for even though no conscious integration or assimilation is reached, he experiences and is ashamed of his shrinking body.

A more profound change occurs in Trueba after Clara cuts off all verbal communication with him. At that time, he no longer tries to force his will upon her but accepts her silence with resignation. Until then, although Clara resisted him, he would not accept the idea that she had choice in the matter of their relations. Even when Clara had a bolt installed on her bedroom door, and told him that since they had nothing to say to each other they would also be unable to share a bed, he argued and "hounded" her. Trueba, arguing that men and women were very different, tried to convince her that, for that reason, it was normal that he could spend all day being furious at her and wish to spend the night making love. Even Trueba, however, admitted that "there was no reason for me to desire her so outrageously."[8]

But after his violence against Clara, even though he instantly begged her forgiveness and tried to make amends, he was forced to recognize that more was broken than Clara's teeth. From that time, he kept his distance, respecting her will and turned his attention toward the political arena. Later, when Trueba, nervous over the coming elections, dares timidly to approach Clara to ask for her infallible predictions, he is no longer the marital tyrant. "'Forgive me, Clara,' he said, blushing like a schoolboy. 'I feel lonely and worried. I'd like to stay here for a while if you don't mind.'"[9]

Although Clara does not speak, they share a silence in good humor and when Clara nods affirmation to the question of whether Trueba will win the election, his response of joy and an affectionate kiss on her forehead seals their new relations. From that time, the hostility between them recedes.

> Clara still said nothing, but he ignored her silence and spoke normally to her, interpreting her slightest gestures as replies. When it was necessary, Clara used the servants or her children to send him messages. She worried about her husband's well-being, helped him with his work, and accompanied him when he asked her to. Sometimes she smiled at him.[10]

Trueba's altered behavior to Clara can be interpreted as recognition that her retreat from him is the price he has to pay for his own excess. If this alteration in Trueba is the result of an increased consciousness, then perhaps it can be argued that some integration of his own femininity has occurred. It is significant that on the night of Clara's death, when he locked himself in her room and lay down next to her to tell her everything he had been holding in since the night he beat her, Trueba realizes that whereas before he had always felt like a giant next to her, now, after his shrinking, they were almost the same size. At least in relation to Clara, Trueba seems to have gained through self-knowledge what he lost in patriarchal supremacy.

In relation to his children, however, as well as in his political activism, there is no evidence of any analogous insight. Having lost his intimacy with Clara, it seems natural that Trueba would turn toward his children for solace, but he has even less success as a father than he had as a husband. The reader cannot help feeling some sympathy for this man who lost the love of a wife he adored, "whose spirit was never with him"; who wanted sons to carry his name and tradition, and had sons who refused both; and who wanted a gentle, loving daughter, and had a daughter who was cold and distant.

On closer inspection, however, one sees that Trueba's disappointment comes from the fact that his children refuse to be what *he wills* them to be. What he derides as failure in his children is precisely their claim to self-assertion. Criticizing and domineering them with the same dogmatism that characterized his political convictions, Trueba engages in power struggles with his children. He struggles for dominance, they for the right to their own self-determination. In this campaign all suffer losses, perhaps Trueba not the least, for he gradually loses all possibility for intimate relationship and is only redeemed through the more genuine love he finds later with Alba, his granddaughter.

Trueba's sons, in their own ways, compensate for their father's dogmatic materialism and political conservatism. Nicholas as a dabbler in spiritualism and Eastern religions, and Jamie as a Socialist medical doctor obsessed with helping the poor. In this way, each son lives out in his own life what in Trueba was never allowed expression. In the end, Trueba disowns his sons for those tendencies, just as he represses them in himself. He ships Nicholas out of the country and drives Jamie to withdraw into a private life, so private that Trueba doesn't believe it when he is later told that Jamie is a close friend of the Socialist President. Thus Trueba's power game with his sons leaves him with his prejudices intact, but at the expense of the loss of any real relation with them.

> Jamie and Nicholas lost what little interest they had in the family and showed no compassion for their father, who in his loneliness tried in vain to build a friendship with them that would fill the void left by a lifetime of bad relationships. They lived in the house because they had nowhere more suitable to eat and sleep, but they came and went like indifferent shadows.[11]

Had he been able to engage in even a minimal receptivity to his sons, Trueba might have led a less isolated and lonely life and perhaps found a better sense of proportion in his political activism. The part he plays in bringing the military dictatorship into power carries a heavy price: the torture and death of his son, rape and torture of his granddaughter, and the betrayal of his country.

Trueba's relationship with his daughter Blanca is even less appealing. Just as he ignores his own poverty of soul, so he ignores the existence of his daughter Blanca. Because she was not the gentle, loving daughter he wanted and because of her attachment to Clara, Trueba loses interest in her. When he does finally take note of her, it is with his violent temper and an uncompromising tyranny. Trueba's reaction to the discovery that Blanca and Pedro Tercero, the revolutionary peasant, are lovers, is immediate and brutal. Blanca is struck with his whip and later forced into marriage with the enigmatic French count whose marriage proposal she had already refused. Moreover, while Clara sensed immediately that there was something dangerous in so much mystery surrounding the count, Trueba's lack of concern reveals a damaged instinct. "For him it was enough that the count was willing to join him in a game of chess or dominoes, that he was clever and friendly and never asked to borrow money."[12]

Once again, then, Trueba's will is done, with catastrophe for all, including himself. Blanca is married to the count, from whom she soon flees in terror and returns to her family home to give birth to Alba, Pedro Tercero's daughter. Although Trueba allows her to return, he never forgives Blanca and from that time on increasingly neglects her, even to the point of not meeting her material needs.

Thus for the second time, Trueba fails with a woman who could have brought light into his inner darkness. Both Clara and Blanca have names symbolic of light, clarity, brightness, but that light never reaches the inner man in Trueba. Instead, after Blanca returns, Trueba grows increasingly rigid and paranoid in his opposition to the rival party, putting all his energy into a political power struggle. In fact, as his inflation grows more and more out of proportion, he becomes more and more a public symbol of his party's conservatism. Were it not for the love which grows between him and Blanca's daughter Alba, he would have become lost in that persona, a public abstraction without any personal connection to the world.

Alba, the third woman whose name suggests light and clarity, is the one who helps to bring Trueba down to earth, both politically and personally. She is a synthesis of Rosa, Clara, and Blanca, more anchored in reality than any of them, even though she has inherited some of Clara's intuitiveness and Rosa's green hair. She also has something none of them had—an easy intimacy and love with Trueba, her grandfather, who was for the first time learning to be happy in a relationship. That love, coming into his life in his old age, was the catalyst that opened the long-repressed feminine soul image of Trueba and brought to him the capacity to understand and forgive both others and himself.

> Esteban Trueba, who had always found it difficult to express his emotions and had had no access to tenderness ever since his relationship with Clara had deteriorated, transferred all his finest sentiments to Alba. The child meant more to him than his own children ever had. Every morning, still in her pajamas, she went to her grandfather's room. She entered without knocking and climbed into his bed. He would pretend to wake up with a start, even though he was actually expecting her, and growled that she should not disturb him and that she should go back to her room and let him sleep. Alba tickled him until, apparently defeated, he permitted her to look for the chocolate he always had hidden for her. Alba knew all his hiding places and her grandfather always used them in the exact same order, but so as not to disappoint him she spent a long time looking, and when she found it she shrieked with joy. Esteban never knew that his granddaughter hated chocolate and that she ate it only out of love for him. Those morning games satisfied the senator's need for human contact. . . . Twice a year he went to Tres Marias with his granddaughter for two or three weeks. They both returned looking tanned, happier, and fatter. . . . At the end of his life, when his ninety years had turned him into a twisted, fragile tree, Esteban Trueba would recall those moments with his granddaughter as the happiest of his whole existence.[13]

Although still assuming patriarchal responsibility for decisions regarding Alba's life, Trueba, somewhat mellowed by the changing times, accepted the fact that "not all women were complete idiots" and even believed that Alba might enter one of the professions—as a second choice, should she fail to attract a well-to-do husband. In that interest, Alba was forced to endure the English school for ten years. But Alba's education also included early years of training in Eastern disciplines with Nicholas, and when she was older, a collaboration with Jamie in his activities in support of the underprivileged classes. Thus compensated by Trueba's two "shadows," Alba's education was not limited by his dominance.

It is through Alba, the narrator at both the beginning and the end, that retribution and resolution finally come for the whole family. Through Alba the consequences of Trueba's actions are brought home, suffered, and finally assimilated. Many threads of the three generations are brought together in Alba's life. The first thread unites Trueba with Alba's parents, Blanca and Pedro, but not before a series of events which reconciles Trueba with both of them. The high point of those events involves a reciprocal rescue of each other by Pedro and Trueba. Pedro Tercero is enlisted by Blanca and Alba to engineer a safe release of Trueba from Tres Marias, where his peasants, under the land reforms of the Socialist regime, had imprisoned him when he attempted to retake the property. The experience, a humiliation for Trueba, was an awkward moment for both, especially since it brought out feelings that neither had expected.

> They stared at each other in silence for several seconds, each thinking that the other was the very incarnation of everything most hateful in the world, but unable to find the old fire of hatred in their hearts.
> "I've come to get you out of here, " Pedro Tercero said.
> "Why?" the old man asked.
> "Because Blanca asked me to," Petro Tercero replied.
> "Go to hell," Trueba said without conviction.
> "Fine. That's where we're going. You're coming with me."[14]

For the first time Trueba experiences a feeling of defeat; and only Alba's love and support help him to regain his dignity.

Later, during the period of the Coup and Terror, Blanca asks her father for help in getting Pedro out of the country. Trueba, in responding to her request, discovers that he could no longer find a single reason for detesting Pedro; his long and passionate hatred had simply dissipated. Moreover, he could no longer feel any of his old anger toward Blanca, who responds to this reconciliation with spontaneous tears, hugs, and kisses. Trueba's rescue of Pedro Tercero repeats the former dialogue between the two men and seals their reciprocal forgiveness.

> "I've come to get you out of here," Trueba said.
> "Why?" Pedro Tercero asked.
> "Because Blanca asked me to," the other answered.
> "Go to hell," Pedro Tercero said.
> "Fine, that's where we're going. You're coming with me."
> The two of them smiled simultaneously.[15]

When Pedro and Blanca prepare to leave the country, the feeling experienced by all three is one of love and reconciliation, and Trueba's last words are a murmured "Go in peace, my children."

This transformation in Trueba would have been impossible without the close and loving connection with Alba which had slowly softened his character. But increased awareness also has its price, as Trueba learns when he is no longer able to escape the fact that he had helped to bring disaster to his country out of the misguided notion that he knew what was best.

According to Jung, the persona and anima have a compensatory relation. He also claims that repression of the anima contaminates the shadow as well. We see these phenomena in the changes which occur in Trueba. As the repressed feminine characteristics begin to emerge in his conscious understanding, both shadow traits and persona are affected. His identification with his political persona weakens at the same time that he becomes aware that he had made wrong choices both in his personal and political relations.

His first moment of truth comes when he can no longer deny that his son was tortured and killed by the military, who were not restoring the country to the conservatives but creating a military tyranny. That is when he begins to think, "I had been wrong to do as I had and that perhaps after all this was not the best way to overthrow Marxism."[16] "For the first time in his life, Senator Trueba admitted he had made a mistake. Sunk in his armchair like an old man at the end of his days, they saw him shed silent tears. He was not crying because he had lost power. He was crying for his country."[17]

When the military police come to drag Alba away with them, Trueba's moment of truth becomes a prolonged agony. He, who had always been self-determining and who had ruled a family, an estate, a country, was unable to protect Alba and was left insulted and helpless by the thugs he had helped bring to power.

But Trueba's moment of truth involved more than that initial brutality of the military; another thread had yet to be drawn into his old age for retribution; other consequences of his former actions had yet to be met through Alba's presence. Those consequences, dating back to the first rape of a young girl on his estate, were brought home to him through the grandson of that girl, Esteban Garcia, now a colonel in the Military. Already with sadistic tendencies and morally twisted as a young boy, Esteban Garcia was tormented by envy of Trueba's legitimate family and had singled out Alba as the instrument of his revenge. To complicate the situation, Trueba had heaped contempt on top of contempt when, in the days of his rage against Pedro Tercero, Esteban Garcia had revealed Pedro's hiding place in return for a promised reward, and Trueba had dismissed the boy with a slap and a snarl, "there's no reward for traitors." Esteban Garcia was never to forget his part in that drama, as Trueba would discover when Alba is made to suffer the consequences of that insult.

In his new helplessness, Trueba finds a self-understanding which is both devastating and liberating and, not least, a new dignity that comes with the acceptance of humility. He accepts the aid of Miguel, Alba's revolutionary lover, as he accepts their pledge of union, no longer finding himself the arbiter of what is right or wrong in others' lives.

On Miguel's advice, he goes to the one person who can help with Alba's release, which brings the final thread into the resolution of his life. That person is Transito Soto, now a financial success and in a favorable connection with the new regime. Transito is the one person toward whom Trueba acted with disinterested generosity, and out of a genuine response to her own wishes for self-determination. And it is Transito who repays his generosity by arranging for Alba's release.

It took four women and a lifetime of struggle for Trueba to finally succeed in "subordinating his libido to the female principle." Until that time it could be said that in him the anima had indeed run away and that violence and tormenting of others followed. Self-knowledge comes late and painfully into his life. In regard to his peasants at Tres Marias, the knowledge comes too late, for, in once more giving way to his violent reactions, he goes too far. With his men spread out, rounding people up with curses, blows, and kicks, Trueba orders the men to burn the peasants' houses and shoot the animals. He dismisses all the tenants with a warning against their ever coming back. But this time Trueba is quick to recognize that he had paid too big a price for his revenge.

> He felt like a father who has punished his children too severely. All that night he kept recalling the faces of the peasants, whom he had seen come into this world on his property, as they moved off along the highway. He cursed his bad temper. Nor was he able to sleep well the rest of that week, and when he finally did he dreamt of Rosa. . . . Disgusted with himself, the *patrón* returned to the city, feeling older than ever. His soul weighed heavy.[18]

Trueba is a complex and provoking character. He exasperates us even as we sympathize with him for having brought himself and others so much misery through his gratuitous and intemperate behavior. Yet, when he comes to Transito to beg for her help in finding Alba, his honesty and lack of false pride win our respect. That humility and the gratitude he shows to Transito is the outer mark of the inner change in him, of his acceptance of his own weakness as well as those of others, and of his new strength—the feminine strength of receptivity and capacity for relationship.

The final reward of that long struggle toward his own completeness is the reconciliation he experiences with the spirit of Clara and the freeing of Alba from any further burdensome consequences of his actions. Alba describes his union with Clara:

> At first she was just a mysterious glow, but as my grandfather slowly lost the rage that had tormented him throughout his life, she appeared as she had been at her best, laughing with all her teeth and stirring up the other spirits as she sailed through the house . . . thanks to her presence Esteban Trueba was able to die happy, murmuring her name: Clara, clearest, clairvoyant.[19]

In regard to her own resolution, and as narrator of the family saga, Alba writes:

> And now I seek my hatred and cannot seem to find it. I feel its flame going out as I come to understand the existence of Colonel Garcia and the others like him, as I understand my grandfather and piece things together from Clara's notebooks, my mother's letters, the ledgers of Tres Marias, and the many other documents spread before me on the table. It would be very difficult for me to avenge all those who should be avenged, because my revenge would be just another part of the same inexorable rite. I have to break that terrible chain. I want to think that my task is life and that my mission is not to prolong hatred but simply to fill these pages while I wait for Miguel, while I bury my grandfather, whose body lies beside me in this room, while I wait for better times to come, while I carry this child in my womb, the daughter of so many rapes or perhaps of Miguel, but above all, my own daughter.[20]

Notes

1. Margaret Ostrowski-Sachs, *From Conversations with C. G. Jung* (Zurich: Juris Druck & Verlag, 1971), 32.

2. Carl Gustav Jung and Marie Louise von Franz, eds., *Man and His Symbols* (New York: Dell Publishing, 1973), 193. Where Self with a capital "S" appears, it refers to Jung's term for the total psyche, both conscious and unconscious.

3. Isabel Allende, *The House of the Spirits*, trans. Magda Bogin (New York: Bantam Books, 1986), 64.
4. Allende, *The House of the Spirits*, 67.
5. Allende, *The House of the Spirits*, 70.
6. Allende, *The House of the Spirits*, 106.
7. Allende, *The House of the Spirits*, 130.
8. Allende, *The House of the Spirits*, 180.
9. Allende, *The House of the Spirits*, 225.
10. Allende, *The House of the Spirits*, 226.
11. Allende, *The House of the Spirits*, 297.
12. Allende, *The House of the Spirits*, 194.
13. Allende, *The House of the Spirits*, 274-75.
14. Allende, *The House of the Spirits*, 360.
15. Allende, *The House of the Spirits*, 393.
16. Allende, *The House of the Spirits*, 377.
17. Allende, *The House of the Spirits*, 390.
18. Allende, *The House of the Spirits*, 386-87.
19. Allende, *The House of the Spirits*, 431.
20. Allende, *The House of the Spirits*, 432.

CHAPTER THREE

A Reluctant Victim of Individuation

Crime and Punishment

> All the greatest and most important problems of life are fundamentally insoluble. They must be so, for they express the necessary polarity inherent in every self-regulating system. They can never be solved, but only outgrown.
>
> The "outgrowing" proved on further investigation to be a new level of consciousness. Some higher or wider interest appeared on the patient's horizon, and through this broadening of his outlook the insoluble problem lost its urgency. It was not solved logically in its own terms, but faded out when confronted with a new and stronger life urge. It was not repressed and made unconscious, but merely appeared in a different light, and so really did become different. What, on a lower level, had led to the wildest conflicts and to panicky outbursts of emotion, from the higher level of personality now looked like a storm seen from the mountain top. This does not mean that the storm is robbed of its reality, but instead of being in it one is above it.[1]
>
> C. G. Jung

The urge and compulsion to self-realization is, says Jung, a law of nature, and thus of invincible power. This is true even when it may seem improbable, given the conscious attitude and behavior of the individual. But the conscious mind is only part of the totality of a person. The far greater part is the unconscious, which has not assignable limits, but which contributes to psychic health and growth through symbolic compensatory messages. According to Jung, it is the task of the conscious mind to understand these hints.

> If this does not happen, the process of individuation will nevertheless continue. The only difference is that we become its victims and are dragged along by fate towards that inescapable goal which we might have reached walking upright, if only we had taken the trouble and been patient enough to understand in time the meaning of the numina that cross our path.[2]

Raskolnikov, a poverty-stricken young man in great inner turmoil who commits a double murder, confesses, and undergoes a conversion in prison, suffers the fate described above. Committed to his belief in rationality and the power of his superior intellect, he fails to see that rationality has its limits and that, when it comes to the crucial decisions in life, reason often proves entirely inadequate. When such a one-sided commitment to rationality leads to a *cul-de-sac,* then, given the power of that urge to self-realization, something happens to the individual which is not a conscious decision.

The transformation which occurs in Raskolnikov at the end of *Crime and Punishment* has caused much controversy among the critics and therefore poses a problem for interpretation.[3] From the point of view of the natural urge and compulsion to self-realization described by Jung, however, Raskolnikov's conversion may be interpreted as a psychological transformation which is at the same time the expression of a religious archetype. Whether we call this transformation a conversion or not, such changes do occur. Jung describes this change as an outgrowing of a narrower level of consciousness toward a new level where the whole outlook of the person is broadened, and it is this broadening which makes the former mode of consciousness—with its problems—lose its urgency. The mode of this transformation varies. Sometimes people outgrow themselves quietly, accepting either from outside or within themselves the possibilities that led to that growth. Sometimes, as in Raskolnikov's case, they are dragged painfully and with great suffering toward those transformations.

From the very beginning we are aware of Raskolnikov as a young man in a state of inner crisis. This crisis is manifested through his state of conflict as he projects two contradictory plans of action. At one moment he is working coolly and rationally on the details of his plan to murder and rob an old pawnbroker. At the next moment he is in anguish and horrified at the very idea of that plan and vehement in his refusal to take that plan seriously. For instance, on his return from an exploratory visit to the old pawnbroker in order to lay concrete plans for the murder, Raskolnikov has a sudden reversal.

> Raskolnikov went out in complete confusion. This confusion became more and more intense. As he went down the stairs, he even stopped short, two or three times, as though suddenly struck by some thought. When he was in the street he cried out, "Oh God, how loathsome it all is! And can I, can I possibly. . . . No, it's nonsense, it's rubbish!" he added resolutely. "And how could such an atrocious thing come into my head? What filthy things my heart is capable of. Yes, filthy above all, disgusting, loathsome, loathsome!—and for a whole month I've been. . . ." But no words, no exclamations, could express his agitation.[4]

On the surface, this seems to be a conventional response of moral revulsion toward the idea of murder. Raskolnikov's moral conflict, however, is by no means a simple-minded conflict of good and evil according to collective norms. Raskolnikov has an acute and profound intellect. He is a modern intellectual who understands contemporary morality as merely shadows of a dead God; consequently he denies its universal validity. In other words, starting from a profound nihilism, Raskolnikov rejects the collective absolutist Christian norm for a relativistic one. At the beginning of the novel, however, he has no consistent hold on his own theories. Moments of clarity are followed by passionate and anguished outbursts. As the novel proceeds, a slow and agonized process of clarification and integration develops until, finally, the internal conflict recedes.

In the beginning, this brilliant university student sees himself as rational, cool, objective, and logical. "Feeling" considerations are deliberately excluded as he examines the pros and cons of the pawnbroker's right to live. She is a parasite feeding on those more worthy than herself, and therefore deserves to die in order that the social body might profit from her wealth. It is all clear, justifiable, and rational. Raskolnikov excludes from his considerations all popular notions of right and wrong as outgrown values of an obsolete morality. With this orientation, however, Raskolnikov cannot cope with the intrusions of passionate "feeling judgments" that break through with an agonizing persistence. His vacillation between conscious logical thought and impassioned "illogical" feeling torments him and makes it impossible for him to interact with other people. The conflict absorbs all his energy, both before and after the murder.

According to Jung's theory of types, Raskolnikov is a "thinking type," dominated by the thinking function, which means that his feeling function is repressed. Jung warns that feeling should not be confused with emotion, for, according to him, feeling is a *rational* function characterized by the making of value judgments. Emotion, in contrast, is more a physiological reaction.

> If you study emotions you will invariably find that you apply the word "emotional" when it concerns a condition that is characterized by physiological innervations ... I take emotion as affect, it is the same as "something affects you." It does something to you—it interferes with you. Emotion is the thing that carries you away. You are thrown out of yourself; you are beside yourself as if an explosion had moved you out of yourself and put you beside yourself. There is a quite tangible physiological condition which can be observed at the same time. So the difference would be this: feeling has no physical or tangible physiological manifestations, while emotion is characterized by an altered physiological condition.[5]

As a thinking type, Raskolnikov's feeling is unadapted, and he therefore lacks the cognition that comes through feeling judgments. Where it is primitive and strongly repressed, feeling tends to intensify until it breaks through as affect or emotion. This can occur because the relation between affect and feeling is a question of degree.

This is what happens to Raskolnikov, whose repressed feelings remain primitive and undeveloped. They are therefore prone to intrude at inappropriate moments into his conscious life. As long as they remain repressed, Raskolnikov is unable to incorporate his feelings into his conscious thought.

In a spontaneous outrage, early in the book, he stops a middle-aged gentleman from taking advantage of a young drunken girl who had obviously just been betrayed. Raskolnikov gives a policeman money to see her safely home and out of the clutches of the man who would profit from her confusion to exploit her. But, as though suddenly "coming to," Raskolnikov reverses himself.

> At that moment something seemed to sting Raskolnikov; in an instant a complete revulsion of feeling came over him. . . . "He has carried off my twenty copecks," Raskolnikov murmured angrily when he was left alone. "Well, let him take as much from the other fellow to allow him to have the girl and so let it end. And why did I want to interfere? Is it for me to help? Have I any right to help? Let them devour each other alive—what is it to me?"[6]

Raskolnikov is confused by his inability to assimilate these unbidden intrusions of feeling. In some cases, as for instance following his dream of peasants beating a horse to death, they cause him great anxiety.

> And Mikolka swung the shaft a second time and it fell a second time on the spine of the luckless mare. She sank back on her haunches, but lurched forward and tugged forward with all her force, tugged first on one side and then on the other, trying to move the cart. But the six whips were attacking her in all directions, and the shaft was raised again and fell upon her a third time, then a fourth, with heavy measured blows. . . . The mare stretched out her head, drew a long breath and died.[7]

In his dream, Raskolnikov, as a little boy, rushes toward the dead mare.

> But the poor boy, beside himself, made his way screaming through the crowd to the sorrel nag, put his arms around her bleeding dead head and kissed it, kissed the eyes and kissed the lips. . . . Then he jumped up and flew in a frenzy with his little fists out at Mikolka. At that instant his father who had been running after him, snatched him up and carried him out of the crowd.[8]

Awakening in terror, Raskolnikov asks himself the meaning of such a dream. That it has significance for him, in some sense, is clear from his immediate associations. "Good God! . . . can it be, can it be, that I shall really take an axe, that I shall strike her on the head, split her skull open . . . that I shall tread in the sticky warm blood, break the lock, steal and tremble; hide, all spattered in the blood . . . with the axe . . . Good God, can it be?"[9]

Some inner warning comes through to Raskolnikov with this dream, because he immediately rejects his plan of murder. "No, I couldn't do it, I couldn't do it! Granted, granted that there is no flaw in all that reasoning, that all that I have concluded this last month is clear as day, true as arithmetic. . . . My God! Anyway I couldn't bring myself to it! I couldn't do it, I couldn't do it!"[10] The liberating effect of that dream is reinforced by the momentary freedom from compulsion which he experiences while standing on the bridge over the Neva.

> He rose to his feet, looked round in wonder as though surprised at finding himself in this place, and went towards the bridge. He was pale, his eyes glowed, he was exhausted in every limb, but he seemed suddenly to breathe more easily. He felt he had cast off that fearful burden that had so long been weighing upon him, and all at once there was a sense of relief and peace in his soul. "Lord," he prayed, "show me my path—I renounce that accursed . . . dream of mine."
> Crossing the bridge, he gazed quietly and calmly at the Neva, at the glowing red sun setting in the glowing sky. In spite of his weakness he was not conscious of fatigue. It was as though an abscess that had been forming

for a month past in his heart had suddenly broken. Freedom, freedom! He was free from that spell, that sorcery, that obsession![11]

But the momentary release coming from the message of the dream is deceptive, for Raskolnikov is not free from his obsession, and all relief slips away when he overhears, in the Hay Market, that Lizaveta, the old pawnbroker's sister, will be away from home at the crucial hour. Taking that unsought information as fated, Raskolnikov again falls into his compulsive idea.

> He was only a few steps from his lodging. He went in like a man condemned to death. He thought of nothing and was incapable of thinking; but he felt suddenly in his whole being that he had no more freedom of thought, no will, and that everything was suddenly and irrevocably decided.[12]

From Dostoyevsky's point of view, what is repressed in Raskolnikov is what, in *Notes from the Underground*, he calls will, or the whole self. "You see, gentlemen, reason is an excellent thing, there's no disputing that, but reason is nothing but reason and satisfies only the rational side of man's nature, while will is a manifestation of the whole life, that is, of the whole human life, including reason and all the impulses."[13] Raskolnikov acknowledges only the intellectual side of himself. But his repressed "whole self" nevertheless torments him with its irrational outbursts. That is Dostoyevsky's description. If, however, we take the repressed feeling judgments as part of the shadow, and the inner voice as coming from the Self, then we can equally well interpret Raskolnikov's self-division in Jungian terms. From this point of view, the process of integration can be described as painful and halting in Raskolnikov. His first important insight comes to him only after he hides the stolen purse and trinkets, when he realizes that, if he were really intending to serve useful social purposes with the old woman's money, he would not have hidden it away without even looking at it. This self-revelation tortures him into confronting his deeper motives, which come to consciousness in a later dialogue with Sonia. At that time he recognizes his real motive for the murder; he only wanted to discover whether he could step over moral boundaries, to see if he were a Napoleon or a louse—"I only wanted to have the daring."[14]

With or without a Jungian interpretation, one can see the polarization of Raskolnikov's repressed spirituality and conscious nihilism externalized in the characters of Sonia and Svidrigailov. But the explanation of his fascination for both is enhanced by seeing them as the bearers of his unconscious projections. As an anima projection, Sonia represents Raskolnikov's "soul image" as well as his feminine side. The anima, when integrated, becomes a bridge to the unconscious, a link to one's hidden side. How does Sonia fulfill this role? As characterized by Jung:

> The anima is not the soul in the dogmatic sense, not an *anima rationalis* which is a philosophical conception, but a natural archetype that satisfactorily sums up all the statements of the unconscious, of the primitive mind, of the history of language and religion. It is a "factor" in the proper sense of the word. Man cannot make it; on the contrary, it is always the *a priori* element in his moods, reactions, impulses, and whatever else is spontaneous in psychic life. It is something that lives of itself, that makes us live; it is a life behind consciousness that cannot be completely integrated with it, but from which, on the contrary, consciousness arises. For, in the last analysis, psychic life is for the greater part an unconscious life that surrounds consciousness on all sides.[15]

Even before he has met her, when he has only heard about her from her father, Raskolnikov recognizes the vital link between Sonia and himself. In fact, he knows before he commits the murder that he will confess to her. He admits this in his first visit to Sonia's room. "I know and will tell . . . you, only you. I have chosen you out. I'm not coming to you to ask forgiveness, but simply to tell you. I chose you out long ago to hear this, when your father talked of you. . . ."[16] Although he resists her profound religious optimism and belief in life, he knows that in the end he will do as she advises and confess his crime, for her spontaneous response to his confession unites him immediately with his repressed feelings.

> "What have you done—what have you done to yourself!" she said in despair, and jumping up, she flung herself on his neck, threw her arms around him, and held him tight. Raskolnikov drew back and looked at her with a mournful smile.
> "You are a strange girl, Sonia—you kiss me and hug me when I tell you about that. . . . You don't think what you are doing."
> "There is no one—no one in the whole world now so unhappy as you!" she cried in a frenzy, not hearing what he said, and she suddenly broke into violent hysterical weeping.
> A feeling long unfamiliar to him flooded his heart and softened it at once. He did not struggle against it. Two tears started into his eyes and hung on his eyelashes.[17]

Sonia speaks to Raskolnikov as a messenger of his own unconscious spirituality, but that voice cannot be heard across the barrier of his intellectual pride. That is why he recognizes his own inner voice as "hers," as something alien to him. There is a natural resistance to the anima, Jung explains, because the anima represents what conscious life has excluded.

One glaring omission in Raskolnikov's self-justification is the problem of Lizaveta, the pawnbroker's sister. Raskolnikov cannot absolve himself of guilt and crime in regard to her murder, since she did not deserve to be murdered and no one would profit from her death. Since her murder does not fit in with his theories, Raskolnikov simply puts her out of his consciousness. It is almost as though he has forgotten that he killed two women instead of one. Only when he is confronting Sonia is he forced to think of her, not only because she was Sonia's friend, but also because he sees Lizaveta's expression in Sonia's eyes. Confronting Sonia, Raskolnikov's barriers weaken.

It is on his second visit to Sonia that Raskolnikov finally becomes conscious of the real motive for the murder. This important passage is the real turning point in his life, for now he is forced to recognize his own shadow side. In Raskolnikov's case, it means seeing himself as a "louse," a term he has up to now reserved for the ordinary people, those who cannot "overstep barriers," who find their morality ready-made. In regard to the shadow, Jung says:

> Everyone carries a shadow, and the less it is embodied in the individual's conscious life, the blacker and denser it is. If an inferiority is conscious, one always has a chance to correct it. Furthermore, it is constantly in contact with other interests, so that it is steadily subjected to modifications. But if it is repressed and isolated from consciousness, it never gets corrected. It is, moreover, liable to burst forth in a moment of unawareness.[18]

According to Jung, recognition of one's shadow side does not automatically guarantee the correction of moral defects. Change only occurs if one chooses to change. That is why recognition of the shadow is a moral problem. Raskolnikov, fascinated by his theories, by the nihilism which underlies his ethical relativism, evades that problem until the very end.

Svidrigailov, as a shadow projection of Raskolnikov, both fascinates and repels him. He recognizes that there is something drawing him to Svidrigailov, but he is not aware that it is his own nihilism, carried to its final limits. Svidrigailov is more consistent than Raskolnikov; he is not torn between two opposing sides of himself because he has surrendered to nihilism. When we encounter him in the novel, he has already reached the point of almost total boredom as the result of a relentless and unscrupulous pursuit of his own desires. Svidrigailov intuits the common link between himself and Raskolnikov long before the latter is willing to acknowledge it.

> He hurried to Svidrigailov's. What he had to hope from that man he did not know. But that man had some hidden power over him. Having once recognized this, he could not rest, and now the time had come . . . could he be expecting something *new* from him, information, or some means of escape? . . . Was it destiny or some instinct bringing them together? Perhaps it was only fatigue, despair; perhaps it was not Svidrigailov but some other whom he needed, and Svidrigailov had simply presented himself by chance . . . he could not help inwardly owning that he had long felt that he must see him for some reason. But what could they have in common?[19]

In ironic amusement, Svidrigailov recognizes the moral bankruptcy to which they have both been led. His self-contempt includes contempt for Raskolnikov, whose self-deception prevents him from facing what has become all too obvious to Svidrigailov. When Raskolnikov confronts Svidrigailov: "If you want to tell me anything—for I keep fancying all this time that you have something to tell me—make haste and tell it, for time is precious and very likely it will soon be too late." Svidrigailov replies:

> Here, you, for instance have come to me not only for a definite object, but for the sake of hearing something new. Isn't that so? . . . Well, can't you fancy then that I, too, on my way here in the train was reckoning on you, on your telling me something new, and on my making some profit out of you! You see what rich men we are![20]

Not until Svidrigailov commits suicide does Raskolnikov acknowledge the fact that the life and death of Svidrigailov are also possible for him. Faced with that realization, Raskolnikov finally chooses the painful task of confession and punishment. At this point, he does not see his choice as a moral choice; it is only a choice for life. Yet the rejection of suicide is to some extent a conscious acceptance of his shadow, since he is now forced to accept responsibility for the Svidrigailov within himself. Assimilation of the shadow, however, does not automatically confer psychic integration nor does it resolve all conflicts. In Raskolnikov's case, the demands of a humiliated ego prevent him from seeing the murder as a crime. He tells his sister Dounia, "I am going at once to give myself up. But I don't know why I am going to give myself up." Denying that he committed a crime in killing the old woman, he says: "I couldn't carry out even the first step, because I am contemptible, that's what's the matter! And yet I won't look at it as you do. If I had succeeded I should have been crowned with glory, but now I'm trapped."[21] What in Christian terms might be called intellectual pride, or the sin of defiance, gnaws too profoundly at Raskolnikov to leave any room for conventional remorse. Aware of his intellectual superiority over the unthinking, hypocritical masses, Raskolnikov is revolted at the thought of their judgment on him. He does not know why he is confessing, although he knows that he will confess. In fact, the compulsion to confess is as strong as the compulsion to commit the crime. What he cannot do is give himself a rational justification for the confession. This is because in identifying with his conscious ego, Raskolnikov has lost his connection with the most profound part of himself. It is only Sonia, his projected soul image, who unites him with that deep Self. He is caught in a familiar Dostoyevskian trap of self-will. By asserting his moral right to the satisfaction of ego desires, he loses his freedom when those desires become compulsions. According to Dostoyevsky, the only escape is through suffering, which leads one back to God's will and genuine freedom in the experience of the full Self. Since the compulsive irrational outbursts come from the whole, but hidden, Self, they cannot be explained by the narrower ego. That is why Raskolnikov cannot understand his own compulsion to confess.

Looked at from a Jungian point of view, the Dostoyevskian transition from a rigid rationality and self-will to freedom and God's will through suffering is comparable to the individuation process. By this means, there is a recentering of the personality, from the ego as center of consciousness to the Self as center of the total psyche, both conscious and unconscious. Until the very end of the novel, Raskolnikov has not made that transition from ego toward Self. Hence it is consistent that from our earliest account of him until his dream in prison, his spontaneous acts of generosity and love, which are motivated by unconscious feeling, are persistently repudiated by his conscious ego. He doesn't know why he is confessing because that action is motivated by feelings he cannot consciously acknowledge. In hindsight, to his conscious mind the murder was stupid and the confession even more stupid. In prison with such self-contempt, Raskolnikov is alienated and withdrawn. But under the surface of consciousness, his conflict continues and intensifies until finally he becomes ill and has a dream that transforms him. What could not break through the rational barrier of his conscious intellect slips in through the imagery of symbols.

> He dreamt that the whole world was condemned to a terrible new strange plague that had come to Europe from the depths of Asia. All were to be destroyed except a very few chosen. Some new sorts of microbes were attacking the bodies of men, but these microbes were endowed with intelligence and will. Men attacked by them became at once mad and furious. But never had men considered themselves so intellectual and so completely in possession of the truth as these sufferers, never had they considered their decisions, their scientific conclusions, their moral convictions so infallible. Whole villages, whole towns and peoples went mad from the infection. All

were excited and did not understand one another. Each thought that he alone had the truth and was wretched looking at the others, beat himself on the breast, wept, and wrung his hands. They did not know how to judge and could not agree what to consider evil and what good; they did not know whom to blame, whom to justify. Men killed each other in a sort of senseless spite. They gathered together in armies against one another, but even on the march the armies would begin attacking each other, stabbing and cutting, biting and devouring each other. The alarm bell was ringing all day long in the towns; men rushed together, but why they were summoned and who was summoning them no one knew. The most ordinary trades were abandoned, because everyone proposed his own ideas, his own improvements, and they could not agree. The land too was abandoned. Men met in groups, agreed on something, swore to keep together, but at once began on something quite different from what they had proposed. They accused one another, fought and killed each other. There were conflagrations and famine. All men and all things were involved in destruction. The plague spread and moved further and further. Only a few men could be saved in the whole world. They were a pure chosen people, destined to found a new race and a new life, to renew and purify the earth, but no one had seen these men, no one had heard their words and their voices.[22]

The dream conveys to Raskolnikov that his nihilism was not a valid picture of the universe, but only a diseased state of his own soul. With this entirely new perspective of the limitations and larger implications of nihilism, he can no longer remain in his former perspective; for the dream has set in motion an inner movement which has altered him. The dream is clearly an "end of the world and re-creation" dream, which speaks to him of his own death and spiritual rebirth. That inner movement can be understood as a movement away from the narrow limitation of his former identification, and signifies an openness to the guidance of the whole Self. The part cannot comprehend the whole. Before this inner movement, Raskolnikov could not consciously comprehend his irrational behavior. Now, in his convalescent state, haunted by the imagery of the dream, he becomes detached from his past, which the dream tells him symbolically was infected with moral disease.

The argument for Raskolnikov's conversion hinges upon the credibility of such an expansion of consciousness, an expansion he has been warding off all through the novel. According to some critics, that "conversion" is out of character; but according to this interpretation, it is the dream which changes Raskolnikov's perspective and moves him psychically to a new orientation, illustrating the fact, described by Jung, that neither the analyst nor the patient *solves* his problems through an intellectual resolution. What does happen is that the patient outgrows his problem, which loses its significance for him because the energy has been withdrawn from it. In writing on the transcendent function, Jung describes this process:

> The shuttling to and fro of arguments and affects represents the transcendent function of opposites. The confrontation of the two positions generates a tension charged with energy and creates a living, third thing—not a logical stillbirth in accordance with the principle *tertium non datur* but a movement out of the suspension between opposites, a living birth that leads to a new level of being, a new situation.[23]

The moment of transformation in Raskolnikov follows the pattern described by Jung when unconscious contents are assimilated into consciousness.

> For the moment I will refrain from discussing the nature of this change of personality, since I want only to emphasize the fact that an important change does take place. I have called this change, which is the aim of our analysis of the unconscious, the transcendent function.[24]

> Natural transformation processes announce themselves mainly in dreams. Elsewhere I have presented a series of dream symbols of the process of individuation. They were dreams which without exception exhibited rebirth symbolism.[25]

It is in these terms that Raskolnikov's transformation can be understood. The problem of dealing with his failure and stupidity in committing the crime and confessing to an action he refused to see as a crime is not resolved. It has simply lost its intensity for him. His energy is now caught up in a blissful experience of feeling and of a new freedom to experience and express those feelings. In this intense experience of newly assimilated feelings, the old problem simply fades out of the center of interest. His spiritual rebirth is synonymous with this assimilation of a part of himself that had been repressed and suppressed; hence he experiences an expansion of life and freedom.

Although the change of personality Raskolnikov undergoes is not a traditional religious conversion, one might call it a religious *experience*. In the language of Dostoyevsky, an ecstatic love for life is a religious experience, perhaps even a necessary preliminary to Orthodox faith.

As the effects of the dream linger with him, Raskolnikov's love for Sonia emerges into his consciousness; and as he admits and accepts his love for her, so does he accept in himself the feminine side of his nature. On that day Raskolnikov experiences himself as open to life and love. A new sense of life and mystery has blown apart his reductionist views of human possibility, and he encounters a whole new side of himself.

> And what were all, *all* the agonies of the past! Everything, even his crime, his sentence and imprisonment, seemed to him now in the first rush of feeling an external, strange fact with which he had no concern. But he could not think for long together of anything that evening, and he could not have analyzed anything consciously; he was simply feeling. Life had stepped into the place of theory and something quite different would work itself out in his mind.[26]

Notes

1. Carl Gustav Jung, *Collected Works* vol. 13, trans. R. F. C. Hull (Princeton: Princeton University Press, 1968), 17-18.

2. Carl Gustav Jung, *Collected Works* vol. 11, trans. R. F. C. Hull (Princeton: Princeton University Press, 1967), 460.

3. The controversy centers upon whether or not Raskolnikov's conversion at the end of the book is artistically or psychologically justified. Ernest J. Simmons does not find it justified and claims that Dostoyevsky was influenced by subjective rather than artistic reasons. E. H. Carr is more lenient, suggesting that to find the ending convincing we have to agree with Dostoyevsky that the way to spiritual strength is through physical suffering. K. V. Mochulsky dismisses the ending as a "pious lie," not to be believed. Richard Peace finds no problem with the ending and claims that it needs no apology.

4. Fyodor Dostoyevsky, *Crime and Punishment*, trans. Constance Garnett (New York: Modern Library, 1950), 7.

5. Carl Gustav Jung, *Analytical Psychology* (New York: Vintage Books, 1970), 26.

6. Dostoyevsky, *Crime and Punishment*, 46.

7. Dostoyevsky, *Crime and Punishment*, 54.

8. Dostoyevsky, *Crime and Punishment*, 54.

9. Dostoyevsky, *Crime and Punishment*, 55.

10. Dostoyevsky, *Crime and Punishment*, 55.

11. Dostoyevsky, *Crime and Punishment*, 55-56.

12. Dostoyevsky, *Crime and Punishment*, 58.

13. Walter Kaufman, ed. *Existentialism from Dostoyevsky to Sartre* (New York: New American Library, 1957), 73.

14. Dostoyevsky, *Crime and Punishment*, 376.

15. Carl Gustav Jung, *Collected Works* vol. 9.1, trans. R. F. C. Hull (Princeton: Princeton University Press, 1969), 27.

16. Dostoyevsky, *Crime and Punishment*, 299.

17. Dostoyevsky, *Crime and Punishment*, 370.

18. Carl Gustav Jung, *Psychology and Religion* (New Haven: Yale University Press, 1966), 93.

19. Dostoyevsky, *Crime and Punishment*, 414-15.

20. Dostoyevsky, *Crime and Punishment*, 420-21.
21. Dostoyevsky, *Crime and Punishment*, 466.
22. Dostoyevsky, *Crime and Punishment*, 488-89.
23. Carl Gustav Jung, *The Portable Jung*, ed., Joseph Campbell (New York: The Viking Press, 1971), 298.
24. Carl Gustav Jung, *Two Essays on Analytical Psychology*, trans. R. F. C. Hull (Cleveland: World Publishing Col, 1967), 232.
25. Jung, *Collected Works* vol 9.1, 130.
26. Dostoyevsky, *Crime and Punishment*, 491.

CHAPTER FOUR

The Rainmaker of Bagdad

Bagdad Cafe

> In a remote village in China a long drought had parched the fields, the harvest was in danger of being lost and the people were facing starvation in the months to come. The villagers did everything they could. They prayed to their ancestors; their priests took the images from the temples and marched them round the stricken fields. But no ritual and no prayers brought rain. In despair they sent far afield for a "Rainmaker." When the little old man arrived, they asked him what he needed to effect his magic and he replied, "Nothing, only a quiet place where I can be alone." They gave him a little house and there he lived quietly doing the things one has to do in life, and on the third day the rain came.[1]
>
> Irene de Castillejo

Bagdad Cafe is a film in which the dialogue is minimal, expressing only the mundane exchanges of daily life. It is the camera which conveys the subtleties and nuances of character, the growing depth of relationship, and the heaviness or lightness of atmosphere.

The dominant theme of this film is magic—which operates on several dimensions. On the most obvious level, it is the sleight of hand with which Jasmin, a foreign lady from Germany, entertains the customers of Bagdad Cafe, an isolated truck stop in the desert. But Jasmin's magic operates on a deeper level as well, for she is the Rainmaker whose presence transforms Bagdad from a disharmonious to a joyful and creative community.

In the parable of the Rainmaker, the village is in a state of disorder, and the Rainmaker has to put himself in order first before the disorder of the village can be corrected. For that reason they must wait three days. Jasmin also encounters a community in trouble. Our first glimpse of her, however, is not of a woman whose own life is in order. On the contrary, she and her overbearing German husband obviously find each other intolerable. Even their car is out of control and the scenes depicting their mutual dislike are shot at oblique and distorted angles. The camera is leveled, however, when Jasmin with calm deliberation takes her airline ticket from a common holder, puts on her hat, lifts her suitcase out of the trunk of the car and begins her solitary path into the unknown. In this way she begins to put herself in order.

Although Jasmin's outward demeanor is calm and reserved, the camera reveals the courage underlying that reserve. For example, when Sal, driving his truck back to the Cafe, stops and asks if she needs help, there is only a fleeting expression of fear on her face, but for that moment one sees that she is a foreigner and lone woman dragging a suitcase on a lonely road in "violent America" with no male protector. The expression is quickly banished, however, and her quiet refusal of help speeds Sal on his way—to her obvious relief. Later, another glimpse of her apprehension is given, when in the face of Brenda's cold hostility, we see her inner vision of cannibals dancing around a huge pot in which she is the helpless dinner.

The scene in which Jasmin approaches the Cafe—owned by the black couple, Brenda and Sal—is the first of many similar confrontations between Brenda and herself. It is through Brenda's eyes that we see this apparition approaching—a fat German hausfrau in a tailored suit, topped with a long feathered Tyrolean styled hat, dragging her suitcase behind her. Brenda squints in disbelief as Jasmin turns toward the Cafe from the hot, dry, deserted highway and walks up to stand silently before her. Brenda, seated on a legless chair against the wall of the Cafe has been crying over the departure of her husband with whom she has quarreled and whom she has ordered to leave. The marital discord between Brenda and Sal is a counterpoint of the previous scene between Jasmin and her husband, Munchgstettner. Brenda looks up and wipes the tears from her face. Jasmin looks down and wipes the sweat from hers. The two women stare at one another—a fat, proper German and a black, disheveled American.

In this way, the first meeting of Jasmin and Brenda reveals both their similarities and their differences. Both have separated in disgust from their husbands and face the challenge of establishing their independence. In their own ways, they both show courage and determination. On Jasmin's approach Brenda stops weeping and takes on the role of proprietor of the motel. Jasmin responds to her brusque manner with quiet dignity.

> Brenda — What can I do for you?
> Jasmin — A room?
> Brenda — Here?
> Jasmin — Yes.
> Brenda — Are you sure?
> Jasmin — Sure.
> Brenda — Are you sure you don't want me to call you a cab?
> Jasmin — No.
> . . .
> Brenda — Did your car break down?
> Jasmin — No car.
> Brenda — No car. Sure. That'll be twenty-five dollars. Cash or charge? How do you wanna pay? Cash . . . or charge?[2]

Jasmin's shy exterior is deceptive. She is in no way intimidated by Brenda's rough manner, even though the image of becoming a dinner for cannibals arises in her imagination. Her solid body and soft but determined voice reinforce the impression of quiet strength. Brenda, more volatile and aggressive, tries to provoke her but fails to ruffle her calm composure. In their interchange, Brenda's rudeness is a challenge that goes unheeded as Jasmin refuses to react in kind. When she asks Brenda where the boss is, and Brenda replies, "I'm the boss," Jasmin smiles and takes out her traveler's checks. Her smile has no effect on Brenda. "You gotta carry your suitcase yourself," Brenda tells her. "We ain't no Grand Hotel."

> Jasmin — The center? It is far?
> Brenda — What center? The shopping center?
> Jasmin — Center of Bagdad?
> Brenda — Oh, this is Bagdad.
> Jasmin — This is all?
> Brenda — This is it!
> Jasmin — Uh-huh.
> Brenda — Uh-huh.[3]

The atmosphere between the two women is guarded and cautious. Although Jasmin says very little, she runs her finger over the dusty and disordered desk at which Brenda sits and looks disapprovingly around her. Brenda conveys her disapproval of Jasmin from the start, feeling justified in her suspicion of a woman who appears from nowhere telling nothing about herself and seeming to have nowhere to go.

But Brenda is at war with everyone. In sharp contrast to Jasmin's calm and unobtrusive presence, Brenda's loud and aggressive voice announces her presence and her displeasure everywhere. She upbraids her husband Sal before everyone in the Cafe for his childish irresponsibility. "You're such a child! Only problem is I got two children. I don't need three." She shouts at her talented pianist son to quit playing the piano. "Your music's drivin' me crazy. It sounds like a sewin' machine."[4]

Brenda *is* the Bagdad Cafe—an overburdened, harassed, unkempt person struggling to keep the business going, haranguing everyone and fighting an obviously losing battle. The cafe-motel is seedy and tired looking; the Bagdad "family" is disintegrating as everyone turns away into separate worlds. Her husband, Sal, has left; Phyllis runs about with a wild-looking motorcycle crowd, while Sal Jr., preoccupied with his music, ignores everyone. Cahuenga, the hired help who tends the counter, retreats into his hammock to sleep. Brenda is left to shoulder the responsibility of running the cafe-motel-gas station herself as well as supervising her children and caring for Sal Jr.'s infant, and she is deteriorating under the strain.

Bagdad is a disordered country, both in its outer condition of dirt, clutter, and neglect and in the inner states of its inhabitants. Only Cox, the aging hippy artist who lives in a trailer on the premises, seems to be in harmony with himself and others. It is not surprising, then, that he recognizes immediately the unique quality of Jasmin.

At his first glimpse of her, crossing the yard and dragging her suitcase to her room, he says, "Hello, Stranger. I like your hat. Really."[5] Cox never fails to show his appreciation of Jasmin, and his eyes light up as he witnesses the gradual flowering of her transformation, which has the simultaneous effect of opening the whole community to a new creativity.

According to Jean Bolen's account of the Rainmaker, after his three-day withdrawal into his quiet little house, he "was back in Tao and then naturally the rain came." Being back in Tao, she explains, means that "I can live optimistically, trusting that there will be enough of whatever is needed."[6] Putting one's inner life in order effects the magic, which results in the restoration of outer order.

The magic works slowly but steadily, as Jasmin's presence in Bagdad is felt by the others. Jasmin puts her own motel room in order first, scrubbing the floors and giving it a thorough cleaning. Her next objective is the motel office and, saying nothing to anyone, choosing her time carefully when Brenda is gone on a shopping trip, she slips quietly past Cahuenga, who is asleep in his hammock behind the counter, and descends upon the dirty and cluttered office. With the ruthless determination of a German hausfrau attacking the Augean stables, she discards all the old, useless, and broken junk which litters the room. Her inner vision flashes on the screen—in her suit and Tyrolean hat, up on the roof, scrubbing the motel sign, perched on the Bagdad water tower, scrubbing and polishing. As the outside heap of discarded junk fills up the garbage container, the office gradually becomes a respectable place of business.

The Bagdad family also gradually transforms under Jasmin's spell. Phyllis, after an initial rude gesture to Jasmin, discovers in her an ally. They laugh together in Jasmin's room as Phyllis tries on Herr Munchgstettner's oversized clothes. Jasmin demonstrates a German folk dance. When Phyllis later introduces Jasmin to Eric, the young man who has pitched a tent near Cox's trailer, Phyllis says to him, "This is my girl friend, Jasmin." With Eric and Jasmin there, Phyllis no longer runs off with her wild-looking friends.

Cahuenga and Jasmin form a cooperative relationship and, with Jasmin there helping him, he no longer retreats into his hammock. With Sal Jr., Jasmin's magic finds fertile ground. In contrast to Brenda's impatience with Sal Jr.'s passion for music, Jasmin encourages him to play and sits beside him, her eyes closed in rapt appreciation. It is a magic moment and Cox, captivated by the sight, draws up a chair to watch.

Only Brenda resists Jasmin's magic. In fact, the more Jasmin transforms the Bagdad, the more hostile Brenda becomes. From the first appearance of Jasmin, Brenda shows her lack of sympathy, treating her with thinly veiled irony, which escalates into somewhat hysterical suspicion when she enters Jasmin's room and discovers it filled with men's clothing and toilet articles. Never considering that there might be a simple explanation (Jasmin took the wrong suitcase when she left her husband), her immediate reaction is to call the sheriff. "Look, there's this woman checked in . . . she's got some weird things in her room. I can't make head or tail of 'em. . . . Look, I think you better come over and check 'em out yourself. The sooner the better."[7] Expecting the sheriff to confirm her suspicions, when, on the contrary, he finds nothing amiss and apologizes to Jasmin for the inconvenience, Brenda is incensed.

> Don't tell me that was it . . . I mean, you gotta be kiddin'.
> Is that all I had you come out here for?
> I don't believe it.
> She shows up outta nowhere, without a car, . . . without a man.
> She ain't got nothin' but a suitcase filled with men's clothing.
> How come? How come she acts so funny like she was gonna stay here forever?
> And with no clothes?
> No, I don't like it! It don't make no sense at all!
> No, no, no, no![8]

Brenda is haunted by a feeling of apprehension concerning Jasmin. Driving into town and unaware of Jasmin's invasion of her dirty office, she succumbs to a persistent intuition that "something is wrong," which is confirmed for her when she returns and finds the clean, orderly office. Exploding in anger, she irrationally insists that Jasmin put all the trash back "just the way it was." Only after her spontaneous anger subsides does she ungraciously acknowledge the improvement to her office.

Brenda's exaggerated hostility to Jasmin can be interpreted as a shadow projection. In regard to the shadow, Jung says that obstinate resistances are usually bound up with *projections*—here the cause of the emotion appears to lie in the *other person*.[9] "Because projections are unconscious, they appear on persons in the immediate environment, mostly in the form of abnormal over- or under-valuations which provoke misunderstandings, quarrels, fanaticisms, and follies of every description."[10] The sheriff, in response to Brenda's outburst, reproaches her: "Brenda, what are you so excited about? I've seen her passport and her airline ticket and they're both okay. She's a tourist. What she wears is her business."

The "shadow," according to Jung, is a term describing our own darker side, hidden from us in the unconscious. It consists of the unattractive characteristics we refuse to recognize in ourselves, as well as sides of our character which, never having been developed, remain primitive and unadapted. Depending on our psychological type, all of us have these unconscious inferiorities. The shadow Brenda projects upon Jasmin is the undifferentiated opposite of her own dominant attitude type. Brenda is quick to react to situations; her responses are spontaneous and uninhibited, while Jasmin, in contrast, responds slowly and deliberately. In Jungian terms, Brenda's attitude is extraverted, Jasmin's is introverted. Given that difference, the cause of Brenda's excessive suspicion of Jasmin can be interpreted as a projection of her own primitive and unadapted introversion. In *Two Essays on Analytic Psychology*, Jung says the following in regard to the two attitude types:

> No man is simply introverted or simply extraverted, but has both attitudes potentially in him—although he had developed only one of them as a function of adaptation.[11]

> The reflective nature of the introvert causes him always to think and consider before acting. This naturally makes him slow to act. His shyness and distrust of things induces hesitation, and so he always has difficulty in adapting to the external world. Conversely the extravert has a positive relation to things. He is, so to speak attracted by them. New, unknown situations fascinate him. In order to make closer acquaintance with the unknown he will jump into it with

both feet. As a rule he acts first and thinks afterwards. Thus his action is swift, subject to no misgivings and hesitations. The two types therefore seem created for a symbiosis. The one takes care of reflection and the other sees to the initiative and practical action.[12]

Von Franz, describing the inferior function in *Jung's Typology*, says that the hardest thing to understand is not your opposite function type, that it is "worse to understand the same functional type with the other attitude."[13] Perhaps that is why Brenda keeps repeating, in her confrontations with Jasmin, "It don't make no sense."

But opposites also attract, and Brenda and Jasmin are drawn to each other even though they misunderstand one another. Jung claims that it is equally indispensable for the introvert to arrive at some form of action not constantly bedeviled by doubts and hesitations, and for the extravert to reflect upon himself, yet without endangering his relationships.[14]

When Cox and the sheriff defend Jasmin, Brenda feels betrayed. She jealously refuses to include Jasmin in the Bagdad "family" and makes a point of her refusal, even to the extent of removing Sal's baby from her arms whenever she finds Jasmin holding him. As the "family" falls more and more under Jasmin's spell, Brenda becomes increasingly irrational in her outbursts, until finally an incident precipitates an enantiodromia. This occurs when, in jealousy over her children's rapport with Jasmin, Brenda storms into Jasmin's room, grabs the baby, and orders her children to leave. "I've had it! And I ain't takin' no more, no way! Now, who the hell do you think you are, lady, huh? Just what is your game? You got somethin' against me? You tryin' to drive me crazy or what? Well, nobody . . . gonna do that to me!"[15] She tells Jasmin, spitefully, "Play with your own kids!" Throughout this storm Jasmin remains silent. When Brenda tells her to play with her own kids, her response is sad and quiet. Looking down at her hands, she says, "I do not have any."

The enantiodromia begins a few moments later when Brenda returns with the baby in her arms, looks at Jasmin still sitting where she left her, and tells Jasmin, sighing: "Look, uh, I didn't mean it that way. I, I don't know what got into me. All the work around here, the kids and everything. And my husband left me a week ago."[16] The reversal is a turning point. From then on, the magic of transformation flows rapidly, changing the Cafe, the people, the very atmosphere. That evening, when Jasmin goes to the Cafe, there is a rebirth of spirit in the air. "Good evening, Miss Jasmin." "Good evening, Miss Brenda."[17]

If the goal of individuation is not for everyone, the path of the Rainmaker is even less so, for it is the rare person who can bring spiritual renewal to others. Irene de Castillejo describes this path of individuation in *Knowing Woman*, and the effect it has upon others.

> Others seem to live more fully for their presence: possibilities of work appear unexpectedly or people offer their services unsought, houses fall vacant for the homeless, lovers meet. Life blossoms all around them without their lifting a finger, and, as likely as not, without anyone attributing to them any credit for the happenings, least of all themselves. Rainmakers are very inconspicuous.[18]

She also points out that the Rainmaker doesn't *cause* the rain to fall; he *allows* it.

> The essence of the Rainmaker is that he knows how to allow. The Rainmaker walks in the middle of the road, neither held back by the past nor hurrying toward the future, neither lured to the right nor to the left, but allowing the past and the future, the outer world of the right and the inner images of the left all to play upon him while he attends, no more than attends, to the living moment in which these forces meet.[19]

She describes the Rainmaker as "on his thread," meaning something very similar to what Jung intended with his description of one's lifeline. To be on our thread is to be in touch with the Self.

> I am using the expression "inner clarity" to mean conscious awareness of being on one's thread, knowing what one knows, and having an ability quite simply and without ostentation to stand firm on one's own inner truth. It is when we are on our vital thread that life happens around us in a way that befits our individual destiny, for we have not interfered. This does not necessarily mean that everything happens as we would like. . . . I believe it is also an empirical fact that life happens more fully around those who are on their thread. So storms hold off or rain falls as is required.[20]

According to de Castillejo, life blossoms around the Rainmaker, who does no more than attend to the present moment—and who communicates more through silence than with words. This describes Jasmin as well. As already noted, life does blossom around her. The Bagdad family becomes a harmonious community; the surroundings become clean and cared for, and the Cafe flourishes. Instead of discord and irritability, there is a harmonious atmosphere of growth and creativity. The second characteristic—attending to the present—is equally applicable. Jasmin is quite content to leave her past behind and shows no apprehension in regard to her future; she responds wholly to the present. For instance, stuck with her husband's suitcase instead of her own, she finds humor in his oversized lederhosen, wears his shirts, and teaches herself from the magic set in his suitcase to perform magic tricks. When she discovers that Bagdad is not a town but only a gas station-motel-cafe, she takes what the situation offers and makes a place for herself there. Jasmin never looks back on her marriage. After Brenda's rude interrogation of her, unperturbed, she goes to her room, removes her wedding ring and settles in to begin her new life. Later, when Brenda discovers her office has been cleaned and turns her explosive wrath on her, Jasmin responds quietly with: "I thought you would like it . . . I thought it would make you happy"; and when Brenda insists that she put everything back the way it was, Jasmin, with the same tranquility, begins to drop papers and trash on top of Brenda's desk. When, moments later, Brenda tells her, "Oh cut it out!" Jasmin looks at her mildly and removes the trash. When the sheriff tells her she must leave the country, Jasmin goes as ordered; but she returns to Bagdad with a green card because it is there that she is "on her thread" and she is faithful to her own inner truth. Finally, in true Rainmaker fashion, Jasmin communicates more with silence than words. Her shy "yes" is repeated often, but for the most part she is a listener, allowing her eyes to speak for her.

Jasmin never attributes the transformations occurring about her to any efforts on her part, nor seeks for any position of dominance or special attention. Her performance with the magic tricks at the Cafe throws her into the spotlight, but that effect was not a motivation for her. She accepts the admiration of her audience without any ego inflation and with a shared delight in the fun of the game. One expects that when it will be time to give up the game, she will do so without looking back, and that she will always be in a present that is open to its own future.

The dramatic change in Brenda's character is also an effect of the Rainmaker who, through her capacity to "allow," has made it possible for Brenda, the extraverted woman of action, to pause for self-reflection. In that pause, Brenda's "moment of truth" forces her to recognize the nature of her irrational projection on Jasmin. Responding to that new awareness, she achieves both a moral victory and the ground for a transformation of character. By withdrawing her unconscious projection on Jasmin, Brenda has released new energy for conscious self-appraisal. The result is that a more receptive side of her character emerges and, no longer fearing Jasmin as a dangerous presence, she can include her as one of the Bagdad family.

According to Jung, such a change in attitude is consistent with the kind of transformation that occurs during the individuation process, when one discovers that what was once a problem is so no longer. One does not really solve one's problems, Jung says, one outgrows them. What might once have caused great consternation simply no longer has the same importance; one's energy and attention are drawn elsewhere. Brenda's energy and attention are now directed in more positive channels, toward the revitalization of Bagdad.

At the same time that Brenda admits Jasmin to the Bagdad family, Jasmin perfects her self-taught conjuring tricks and brings her magic to the delighted customers of the Cafe. Soon rain falls in torrents upon Bagdad—in the form of good will, friendship, and laughter. In one scene, Jasmin pulls a flower out of the air and offers it to Brenda, a transformed Brenda, no longer angry, sullen, unkempt, but a gracious and smiling collaborator. Nor is Jasmin the same shy, cautious stranger who wandered into Bagdad. Now one of the Bagdad family, this former introvert charms everyone with her humor and playfulness. Everything has lightened and loosened in her appearance; her clothes, her hair, her smile, all reflect the birth of new energies.

But all fairy tales need their evil days, and Bagdad's day arrives with the return of the sheriff who informs the family that Jasmin's tourist visa has expired. Upon this pronouncement Jasmin and Brenda stand once more facing one another silently, this time sharing the grim realization of their pending loss.

What goes around comes around. Brenda's former attempt to get rid of Jasmin with the help of the sheriff finally succeeds, but now no one, especially Brenda, welcomes this outcome. "Goodbye, Miss Brenda." "Bye, Miss Jasmin." Brenda watches in sorrow as Jasmin crosses the highway with her suitcase.

Without the Rainmaker, Bagdad sinks back into its former torpor. Sal Jr. sadly plays the piano, his baby beside him tied into its highchair. Cahuenga is back in his hammock. A trucker, approaching the now empty Cafe says, "What happened to the magic?" "The magic?" says Cahuenga, "It's gone."

Outside, the camera follows once again Eric's toss of the boomerang, which he taught both Phyllis and Jasmin to sail around the water tower; but now—for the first time—it fails, moves downward, hits the tower, and falls to the earth. The magic is gone. In her office, Brenda watches the fall of the boomerang. She lowers her head sadly.

The bereft family of Bagdad console themselves by hanging a portrait of Jasmin, painted by Cox, on the wall of the Cafe. It is Jasmin in her suit and Tyrolean hat, a compact little German woman whose fey quality of mystery and innocence has been captured in the painting. Cox places a flower in a cup and puts it in front of the portrait, which has become a sort of shrine. The flower motif is repeated throughout the film. Jasmin has the name of a flower; she uses flowers as props for her magic tricks; she holds a single flower in the series of increasingly sensual portraits of her painted by Cox, and he brings wild flowers when, in the final scene of the film, he proposes to her. In a more general sense, it is Jasmin the Rainmaker who makes possible the spiritual flowering of Bagdad; and her banishment brings back the drought, but not entirely, because her memory, her portrait, the "shrine," keep thoughts of her alive.

Most fairy tales, however, have happy endings, and so does Bagdad Cafe. The Rainmaker comes back with her green card, to become a permanent member of the family.

One of the most moving scenes in the film occurs when Jasmin returns and Brenda sees her coming once more across the dusty road with her suitcase. Jasmin, looking happy and youthful, is now hatless and in a white dress. The new Brenda smiles and hurries out joyfully to meet her halfway. Again the two women face each other silently, but now the scene is bright with new life. They hug one another, pause once more to face each other, then hug again in a loving embrace. It is another magical moment with the white German and black American women united in a loving sisterhood, each having discovered a hidden part of themselves through the encounter with the other. As the whole family rushes to welcome Jasmin, Bagdad is once more "on its thread."

Jasmin's return is celebrated by everyone, including thirty-seven truckers, in an extravaganza, more fantasy than reality, in which everyone sings and dances. Brenda and Jasmin do a magical song and dance act with self-moving canes; Sal Jr., with Brenda beaming approvingly at him, plays the piano, and Phyllis sings and dances while Cox and Eric work the spotlights. Even Sal Sr. returns to join the fun. Meanwhile the crowd chants repeatedly, "Magic! Magic! Magic!"

This scene, with Jasmin and Brenda in Las Vegas style costume and routine is a bit overdone, but presumably it is meant to convey life, vitality, and success, especially as a prognosis of the future for the Cafe. The final scenes are better. They recapture Jasmin the Rainmaker, unassuming and attentive. The film ends with Cox, desert flowers in hand, calling on Jasmin in her motel room. Nervously, Cox stumbles through a marriage proposal to Jasmin, prefacing it with the information that if she were to marry an American citizen she would have no visa problems. To all his comments, Jasmin replies, "Yes."

> Cox — uh, . . . if I asked you . . . uh, to marry me.
> Jasmin — Yes?
> Cox — And if you said, "yes" . . . you could stay here forever.
> Jasmin — Yes.[21]

Cox finally puts his proposal bluntly: "Will you marry me, Jasmin?" Jasmin smiles, nods her head, and says, "I'll talk it over with Brenda." It is significant that Jasmin says "Brenda" and not "Miss Brenda," announcing the new intimacy appropriate to sisterhood.

The Rainmaker's work is done, and Bagdad is saturated with happiness. Sal Sr. has returned to Brenda; Jasmin and Cox will share a creative life of inner clarity; Bagdad Cafe's future is secure, and Brenda and Jasmin have established a sisterhood where each can help the other to uncover and live out the less developed sides of themselves. Bagdad Cafe ends in an orgy of individuation.

Notes

1. Irene Claremont de Castillejo, *Knowing Woman* (New York: Harper Colophon Books, 1973), 131-2. The story of the Rainmaker was told to Jung by Richard Wilhelm, who also introduced him to *The Secret of the Golden Flower*. Jung retold the Rainmaker story in *Mysterium Coniunctionis,* and it is often referred to by Jungian analysts and writers.

2. Script for *Bagdad Cafe*, Island Pictures, written and produced by Eleonore Adlon and Percy Adlon (Los Angeles: pelemele FILM GmbH production, 1987), 27-9.

3. Script for *Bagdad Cafe*, 31.

4. Script for *Bagdad Cafe*, 17.

5. Script for *Bagdad Cafe*, 32.

6. Jean Shinoda Bolen, *The Tao of Psychology* (San Francisco: Harper & Row, 1979), 99.

7. Script for *Bagdad Cafe*, 45-46.

8. Script for *Bagdad Cafe*, 53.

9. Carl Gustav Jung, *Collected Works* vol. 9.2, trans. R. F. C. Hull (Princeton: Princeton University Press, 1951), 9.

10. Carl Gustav Jung, *Two Essays on Analytical Psychology*, trans. R. F. C. Hull (Cleveland: World Publishing Co., 1967), 106.

11. Jung, *Two Essays on Analytical Psychology*, 66.

12. Jung, *Two Essays on Analytical Psychology*, 65.

13. Marie-Louise von Franz, *Jung's Typology* (New York: Spring Publications, 1971), 52.

14. Jung, *Two Essays on Analytical Psychology*, 69.

15. Script for *Bagdad Cafe*, 90, 91.

16. Script for *Bagdad Cafe*, 92.

17. Script for *Bagdad Cafe*, 93.

18. de Castillejo, *Knowing Woman*, 132.

19. de Castillejo, *Knowing Woman*, 133.

20. de Castillejo, *Knowing Woman*, 137.

21. Script for *Bagdad Cafe*, 122-123.

PART TWO: COLLECTIVE PATHS

CHAPTER FIVE

The Life of the Spirit in Modern Man: Feast or Famine?

My Dinner With André

The man whom we can with justice call "modern" is solitary. He is so of necessity and at all times, for every step towards a fuller consciousness of the present removes him further from his original *"participation mystique"* with the mass of men—from submersion in a common unconsciousness. Every step forward means an act of tearing himself loose from that all-embracing, pristine unconsciousness which claims the bulk of mankind almost entirely.... Only the man who is modern in our meaning of the term really lives in the present; ... he alone finds that the ways of life which correspond to earlier levels pall upon him. The values and strivings of those past worlds no longer interest him save from the historical standpoint. Thus he has become *unhistorical* in the deepest sense and has estranged himself from the mass of men who live entirely within the bounds of tradition. Indeed, he is completely modern, only when he has come to the very edge of the world, leaving behind him all that has been discarded and outgrown, and acknowledging that he stands before a void out of which all things may grow.[1]

C. G. Jung

My Dinner With André is an anti-film, a film which has no action, no plot, no special effects, and only three male actors. It is a conversation between two men, a spontaneous and disturbing conversation, in which the viewer becomes a silent participant. Both men are part of the New York theatrical world, André, a director, and Wally, a playwright and sometime actor. They are very different types. Their meeting for dinner at a restaurant is the occasion of a reunion during which André gives Wally a bizarre account of the past few years of his absence from New York. That account, which both repels and fascinates the viewer, is a description of a life without ballast, without the restraints and limitations of conventional existence. Wally, a short, stocky, easy-going contrast to the intense and troubled André, responds for the most part with "uh huh," and "wow," and "right," an appropriate response to what sounds only too often like the confessions of a madman.

It is not until the latter part of the film that Wally participates in what becomes a real dialogue, when he brings his grounded, practical, and common-sense views to challenge André's intuitive, symbolic, and esoteric interpretation of his experiences. That dialogue, an attempt at mutual understanding, ends inconclusively but provocatively, both in its description of contemporary life and its projection of a future. The film is dominated by the psychic turmoil of André, and his expression of the spiritual vacuum of contemporary life, an account which concretizes much of what Jung has described in "The Spiritual Problem of Modern Man." According to Jung, modern man has suffered a psychological shock which has thrown him into profound uncertainty. "Although," he says, "we are the culmination of the history of mankind . . . we are also the disappointment of the hopes and expectations of the ages."[2]

What Jung is pointing out here is the moral and political failure of modern man who, in spite of his technological and scientific achievements, cannot succeed in creating a world of peace and harmony. Being aware of this failure, he feels profound uncertainty. Jung also claims that, although the *facts* that are the subject matter of psychology have long been known, it is our spiritual need that has led to our contemporary "discovery" of psychology.

> Psychic life always found expression in a metaphysical system of some sort. But the conscious, modern man, despite his strenuous and dogged efforts to do so, can no longer refrain from acknowledging the might of psychic forces. This distinguishes our time from all others. We can no longer deny that the dark stirrings of the unconscious are effective powers—that psychic forces exist which cannot, for the present at least, be fitted in with our rational world-order.[3]

That we are fascinated by the unconscious and our own subjectivity can be readily seen in the literature of our time, our theater, movies, television productions, and especially in the emphasis we put upon crime and psychopathology. According to Jung, there is no real spirituality in this fascination with the unconscious; nor does he find any spirituality in Western religions. The religions, Jung says, have become something modern man "tries on and lays aside again like worn-out clothes."[4] They no longer fill a spiritual need in us. Instead, our preoccupation with what transcends consciousness is expressed in other unorthodox ways; in astrology, the tarot, the I Ching, past-life regressions, and all sorts of experimenting with Eastern and Native American practices. Jung compares this profusion of activity with the flowering of Gnostic thought in the first and second centuries after Christ. Because these pursuits engage the psychic energy which is no longer invested in obsolete forms of religion, Jung claims that these movements have a truly religious character. Contrary to the traditional religions, these contemporary movements place a priority on subjective psychic experience. The expectation is that, through one's own experience, one can discover what lies in the depths and heights of the psyche. Yet answers are not so easily forthcoming. From the outer side of life, we are already faced with uncertainty. The world the physicist leaves us is becoming more and more volatile; belief in absolute values, whether religious, political, or ethical, has long ago faded and left us with an uncomfortable relativism. "It is no wonder," Jung says, "if the modern man falls back upon the reality of psychic life and expects from it that certainty which the world denies him."[5]

Spiritually we are in a precarious situation, especially since we cannot live without assigning values and meaning. "When our values are destroyed, the psyche will seek some equivalents."[6] But how shall we go about finding them, and how do we choose among them? If it is from our own psychic depths that new spiritual forms will arise, then we have to be able to handle that influx without inundating our ego with forces it cannot handle. That danger is one which André faced and struggled with, and which he describes to Wally.

Our introduction to the film is given through the voice of Wally as he is seen walking through the streets of New York on his way to the dinner engagement. We learn that he is thirty-six, grew up in New York, and lives happily with his girlfriend Debby. We also learn that he had been avoiding his friend André for years, not wanting to deal with whatever terrible thing had led to André's dropping a successful career as theater director to go wandering off for unknown reasons in strange parts of the world.

Wally, apprehensive over the prospect of sticking through an entire meal with André, "who looked crazy" to him, decides to make the evening endurable by letting André talk about what he had been doing the past few years. At first reluctant, André finally begins a long rambling tale of his adventures, beginning with his account of an unorthodox workshop in a forest in Poland. When he was asked to do the workshop, he claims, his state of mind was bleak. "And I had told him that I didn't want to come, because, really, I had nothing left to teach. I had nothing left to say. I didn't know anything, I couldn't teach anything. Exercises meant nothing to me anymore."[7] His experience in Poland, contrary to expectation, was revitalizing, not in the sense of ordinary theater practice, but as the occasion for an exploration of his own inner being. The basis of these workshops, André says, is to "create some terrible hole that we would all drop into. And that's usually quite frightening, because we don't know where we will be at the next moment." The difference from ordinary theater is that in these improvisations the goal is not some character one is seeking, but oneself.

His discussion of that workshop evokes, for the viewer, a mixed response. The description of primitive dancing, chanting, singing, along with gratuitous actions, is somewhat alienating, probably because it represents a communal surrender to something that seems atavistic, what Jung calls *participation mystique*, unconscious identification with a collective. Since, in an evolutionary sense, we are progressing from that state toward a more personal centered consciousness, the return to a more primitive communal unconsciousness can appear threatening. At the same time, however, there is something liberating in that descent since it is in the deep unconscious that our creativity has its source. As a result, the experience is at the same time ambiguous and full of significance.

André insists that the workshop allowed him to know for the first time "what it means to be truly alive." He also admits, however, that most of the people he met at that time thought there was something wrong with him. If the forest experience made him feel "truly alive," the implication is that André must have been missing something very vital to life. At this point in the film one wonders whether André may not be confessing to a purely personal disorder. It also seems questionable whether a retreat into an atavistic expression of communal unconsciousness could be liberating or in any way an evolutionary advance in consciousness. It is only later, when society as a whole is put in question, that the experience he describes gains a new dimension. Every age has its own unconscious participation and André argues that our present collective participation is an unconscious mechanical torpor-like condition of evading and refusing any spontaneous acknowledgment of our deeper feelings. The deliberate descent into a more primitive mode of unconscious participation is what he claims can break the spell of that torpor, of the robot quality of our contemporary communal unconsciousness. Aniela Jaffé, in *The Myth of Meaning in the Work of C. G. Jung*, explains this phenomenon:

> Because the primitive is so close to nature, the meaning of his myths gives him a sense of security. Everything he does, everything he experiences, is intimately connected with the cosmos, with the stars and the wind, with sacred animals and gods. Modern man, with his incomparably more differentiated consciousness, has lost touch with nature both without and within, with his psychic images and therefore with meaning. He is one-sided, and he goes on developing one-sidedly along the path of intellectual differentiation. . . . Contact with the unconscious, which heals and makes whole, restores the connection with his origin, with the source of psychic images. This is not a reversion to barbarism, but regeneration through a renewed and conscious relationship with a living spirit buried in the unconscious. Every step forward on the way to individuation is at the same time a step backwards into the past, into the mysteries of one's own nature.[8]

The contemporary man who dares to surrender himself in that way is released from the deadening form of what has begun to pall upon him, but at the same time, by uprooting himself from his time, he pays the price of alienation from his society.

André describes a series of synchronistic events he experienced at that time which focused upon some hidden connection he felt with Saint-Exupéry's book, *The Little Prince*, but as he himself admits, he was in a peculiar state then—hallucinating, exhausted, weak.

In *Depth Psychology and a New Ethic*, Erich Neumann points out that it is a mistake to take everything which comes from the inner voice as though it were an oracle. What comes from the unconscious should never be automatically accepted. A critical consciousness has to accompany any openness to the unconscious, so that each can be a check on the limitations of the other. Jung also points out the dangers of an uncritical attitude:

> The unconscious functions satisfactorily only when the conscious mind fulfills its tasks to the very limit. . . . If the unconscious really were superior to consciousness it would be difficult to see wherein the advantage of consciousness lay, or why it should ever have come into being as a necessary element in the scheme of evolution.[9]

André's description of his response to the series of synchronicities he experienced indicates that he uncritically surrendered to the inner voice; hence his disastrous trip to the Sahara, a trip which added to his disorientation. "I met this young Japanese Buddhist priest named Kozan . . . I thought he was the Little Prince. And so naturally I decided to go to the Sahara desert to work on *The Little Prince* with two actors and this Japanese priest."[10] With hindsight, André recognizes his vulnerability at that time and tries to explain to Wally that power of the unconscious.

> It's possible that in certain periods of your life the unconscious can have an enormous amount of power, so that it can actually make manifest what you need at that time. It can simply give you signs, make people appear, give you the feeling that you're—that there are so many coincidences that you must be on the right path. In fact, you could be on the wrong path.[11]

André's travels took him to India, back to Long Island, to Findhorn—a new age community in Scotland—to Belgrade, and so on, all the time hallucinating and unable to find any solid ground. His last "big event" was a Halloween eve experience on Long Island, where he and nine others were "buried and resurrected." Following that event he came to the realization that he "just didn't want to do those things any more." As he describes it, his descent into the unconscious was self-limiting. He decided soon afterward to return to New York and to his profession as theater director. What motivated the return to ordinary life? No answer is given. What is significant, however, is the transformation of character that André claims as the outcome of those years, especially a liberation of spontaneous and honest feeling that brought him to very different valuations of individual people, his work, and society in general.

It is at this point, where the focus turns from André's self-exploration toward an analysis of contemporary society, that the dialogue with Wally begins.

André's criticism of contemporary society includes a self-criticism—that we live mechanically, distracting ourselves from any genuine awareness of ourselves, of others, and of our reactions to others. He describes his new and painful reaction to an evening with an old friend of whom he had been fond and whom he can *now* see as a pompous, unconscious, hollow person, telling the same stories over and over again about his famous mother. Prior to his new orientation he would have described a nice evening with the man, not even recognizing that he had been miserable with him.

> You know, if you *admit* to yourself that you just spent an evening with someone and for some reason or another on that particular evening they were somehow driving you insane, then I think you immediately begin to feel some kind of sympathy for that person, and you begin to wonder how he came to be in the state he's in. But we don't admit those things to ourselves. We just bottle everything up. I mean, really, we're just going around all day

like unconscious machines, and meanwhile there's all this rage and worry and uneasiness just building up and building up inside us.[12]

André points out another type of behavior he finds absolutely abnormal, although typical in us—that we cannot honestly confront one another when anything serious or tragic is in question. He cites his own case; two weeks after his mother died, he went out to dinner with three close friends. The evening was spent with everyone joking and laughing when, in fact, he was feeling desperately in need of someone to speak to him about her death. In the same way, he adds, no one will seriously discuss our situation in the world, so that we can act appropriately. Instead, everyone is concerned with how well they are performing. Everyone is just caught up in trying to live up to "someone's fantasy of how a father, single person, or an artist should look and behave," yet privately they don't know what they should be doing with their lives. "No one says what they're really thinking about; they don't talk *to* each other; because I think people are really in some sort of state of fear or panic about the world we're living in, but they don't know it . . ."[13]

As for the theater, André claims it has lost its power to awaken people since the picture of the world it gives—violence, terror, shocking sexual events—are exactly the same as our everyday world, and the result of such theater is to deaden even more an audience already passive and impotent. The theater merely confirms the depressing picture of a world that seems to offer no hope. What André wants from the theater is something that is positive, that will bring an audience to life. On the whole, then, what André sees as the communal unconscious of our time is our inability to really see one another, to know what we are feeling, and to interact on that basis.

Despairing of how to bring about these changes, changes which in himself necessitated that retreat of several years, André speculates on the possibility of a more permanent retreat in the face of a whole world going in the direction of robot unconsciousness. He cites the Findhorn people as among those who believe that laws of nature are at work to balance the present deadness; that as the world grows darker and colder, in different parts of the world new "reserves," islands of light and warmth, will grow and maintain the species, as monasteries did during the Dark Ages. He suggests that through those islands of light a new kind of perception and unity with all things will grow, to send the human species on to a new kind of being.

In the discussion regarding contemporary society, especially the inability of people to really see and hear one another, Wally agrees with André, adding his own observations, for example, that the theater has become superficial and that people "go crazy" if one tries to engage them in any serious discussion. But when André goes on at length about the negative influence of electric blankets, after Wally mentions how different it is to sleep with one, Wally, far from being intimidated, asserts unequivocally his pleasure in it. His unabashed honesty in valuing that simple material comfort has the effect of pulling us back to the commonplace, at the same time making us aware of having been in a somewhat rarefied atmosphere. Going from André's world of dramatic and emotional highs and lows to Wally's electric blanket is a very rapid descent; but Wally makes it clear that he prefers being at ground level. Although he agrees with André that people need to be awakened, he does not agree that everyone needs to be "taken to Mount Everest"—to go through what André experienced in order to break the spell of that communal unconsciousness. Why not, he argues, find reality right here in New York? New York is not less real. What needs to be changed, Wally says, is the mode of one's perception. If one could be brought to perceive correctly, it would be unnecessary to go to Mount Everest, even absurd. Where Wally becomes most adamant is in response to André's claim that civilization has to be preserved through little islands of culture. Wally's "back to earth" objections are not inappropriate; they occur in response to André's description of a roof at Findhorn, constructed so that it could "rise to meet friendly UFO's." When Wally insists that his *actual* response to all that is that he's just trying to earn a living, pay the bills, and enjoy a simple life with Debby, he has the viewer's sympathy.

Wally insists that we don't need to move to some esoteric outpost to find life meaningful; that there are simple pleasures in life that we can enjoy. He also finds objectionable André's rejection of Western civilization.

> Even if I *did* feel the way you do—you know, that there's no possibility for happiness now—then, frankly, I *still* couldn't accept the idea that the way to make life wonderful would be to totally reject Western civilization and to fall back into a kind of belief in some kind of weird something.[14]

It is the atavistic quality of André's experience that Wally most objects to. "I read fortune cookies too," Wally says, "but in my *conscious* mind I know it's a joke." Wally's criticism is appropriate, since the inability to use conscious discrimination effectively is André's weakness. André defends himself with the admission that what it all meant was that he had entered the unconscious, and that he recognizes now the danger of such surrender.

> *I* think what it means to be involved in those things in a way is that you've entered the unconscious, that you're in the world of the unconscious, and that to some extent your ego has gone, or your ego base has dissolved, and in that sense, I mean, you're in the underworld. And you can actually begin

to think that you have the unconscious ability to make signs or omens happen, and you can get very excited by it because I guess you think you have some kind of power. And that's disturbing. I mean, you know, following omens and so on is probably just a way of letting ourselves off the hook so that we don't have to take individual responsibility for our own actions. After all, it's not easy for us to make our own decisions, because our knowledge of ourselves is too limited. . . . And I agree with you that that is frightening. I mean, and giving yourself over to the unconscious can leave you vulnerable to all sorts of very frightening manipulation. And in all the work that I was involved in, there was always that danger.[15]

In his defense, however, André makes an observation that is very similar to Jung's point in "The Spiritual Problem of Modern Man." André says:

But the thing is, Wally, I think it's the exaggerated worship of science that has led us into this situation. I mean, science has been held up to us as a magical force that would somehow solve everything. Well, quite the contrary. It's done quite the contrary. It's destroyed everything. So that is really what has led to this very strong, deep reaction *against* science that we're seeing now . . .[16]

Jung's comments are the following:

The modern man has lost all the metaphysical certainties of his mediaeval brother, and set up in their place the ideals of material security, general welfare and humaneness. But it takes more than an ordinary dose of optimism to make it appear that these ideals are still unshaken. Material security, even, has gone by the board, for the modern man begins to see that every step in material "progress" adds just so much force to the threat of a more stupendous catastrophe. The very picture terrorizes the imagination.[17]

André also concedes that one doesn't have to be taken to Mount Everest to come awake. He admits that *he* needed that training program to learn how to be a human being, that he had to cut out all the noise around him, stop performing, and listen to what was inside him. "Now maybe in order to do it, you have to go to the Sahara, and maybe you can do it at home. But you need to cut out the noise."[18] Implicit in André's messianic drive toward leading people to "cut out the noise" and to listen to the silence within themselves is the belief that humanity is at a turning point and that the possibility for a new start for humanity has to begin with a transformation of the individual. In other words, it is up to each person, individually by his efforts with himself, to change the world. This belief is consistent with what Jung claimed, that personal individuation is not separate from collective individuation since the spirit of the age realizes itself in the individual. This need characterizes our time, because we have grown disillusioned with collective political movements and our cynicism has deadened our sensibility. Our expectation that some rational organization of the world will bring peace and harmony has, as Jung says, "grown pale." The modern man's scepticism regarding all such matters has chilled his enthusiasm for politics and world-reform.

Thus modern man has been thrown back upon himself; but what distinguishes our time from all others, according to Jung, is our fascination with the unconscious, with its power, and with the fact that, up to now at least, we cannot fit it in with our rational world order. André is struggling with that challenge and in that sense he is a "modern" man.

André and Wally both make concessions. What they agree upon is the need for change, for a more real and genuine self-encounter and relation with others. André is more insistent that the route to this renewal is through the unconscious. His strong faith in this mode of renewal is at one with Jung's contention that the modern age will find its direction from the new spiritual forms it finds in the depths of the psyche.

The dialogue ends inconclusively both in its prescription for what ails modern man and in its prognosis for the future. Nor does Jung make any specific predictions regarding our "spiritual problem"; he only points out the form it takes:

> It seems to me that we are only at the threshold of a new spiritual epoch. . . . It is from need and distress that new forms of life take their rise, and not from mere wishes or from the requirements of our ideals.
>
> To me, the crux of the spiritual problem of today is to be found in the fascination which psychic life exerts upon modern man. If we are pessimists, we shall call it a sign of decadence; if we are optimistically inclined, we shall see in it the promise of a far-reaching spiritual change in the Western world.[19]

The film leaves us with Wally on his way home to Debby, again with Wally's over-voice and a return to the commonplace as he recognizes the streets of New York that were significant in his childhood.

Form and content meet in this film. In the dialogue, both Wally and André affirm their desire to awaken their audience and to leave them with something positive. The unorthodox experiment of a film with two actors, one a director and the other a playwright, doing nothing but talk through a dinner is undoubtedly part of the plan to shake us out of our habitual expectations as audience. Furthermore, we have before us a concrete example of what the dialogue is all about—two people who are awake enough to really listen to each other, who talk seriously, and who respond to what they hear. The rest is up to the audience.

Notes

1. Carl Gustav Jung, *Modern Man in Search of a Soul*, trans. Delland Baynes (New York: Harvest Book, Harcourt Brace and World, 1933), 197.
2. Jung, *Modern Man in Search of a Soul*, 199.
3. Jung, *Modern Man in Search of a Soul*, 203.
4. Jung, *Modern Man in Search of a Soul*, 206.
5. Jung, *Modern Man in Search of a Soul*, 213.
6. Jung, *Modern Man in Search of a Soul*, 215.
7. Wallace Shawn and André Gregory, *My Dinner With André, A Screen Play for the Film by Louis Malle* (New York: Grove Press, 1981), 22.
8. Aniela Jaffé, *The Myth of Meaning* (New York: Penguin Books, 1975), 148-49.
9. Carl Gustav Jung, *Collected Works* vol. 8, trans. R. F. C. Hull (Princeton: Princeton University Press, 1964), 296.
10. Shawn and Gregory, *My Dinner With André*, 41.
11. Shawn and Gregory, *My Dinner With André*, 46.
12. Shawn and Gregory, *My Dinner With André*, 63.
13. Shawn and Gregory, *My Dinner With André*, 68.
14. Shawn and Gregory, *My Dinner With André*, 98.
15. Shawn and Gregory, *My Dinner With André*, 101-2.
16. Shawn and Gregory, *My Dinner With André*, 103.
17. Jung, *Modern Man in Search of a Soul*, 204.
18. Shawn and Gregory, *My Dinner With André*, 109.
19. Jung, *Modern Man in Search of a Soul*, 217.

CHAPTER SIX

Rebirth, Prophecy, and the Big Dream

Novels of Dostoyevsky

> To concern ourselves with dreams is a way of reflecting on ourselves—a way of self-reflection. It is not our ego-consciousness reflecting on itself; rather, it turns its attention to the objective actuality of the dream as a communication or message from the unconscious, unitary soul of humanity.[1]
>
> C. G. Jung

The psyche, according to Jung, is a self-regulating mechanism, in which dreams play a significant part in correcting attitudes that are too one-sided or limiting. They can do this because thoughts and inclinations which have been too little valued in conscious life come into action spontaneously during the sleeping state. With the conscious process largely eliminated, the dream can add to the situation all aspects essential for a different point of view. The dream may even be describing a situation in total opposition to consciousness. In this way the dream broadens a too narrow perspective so that a transformation of attitude becomes possible. This is the compensating function of dreams. Since most dreams are compensatory, in order to understand them one must know something about the conscious situation. Even knowing that, however, may not guarantee an understanding of the dream. Dreams speak in the language of symbols. Although these symbolic messages coming from the deep unconscious make no sense in terms of our ordinary logic, they reach us in another way, through a "logic" of association, the language of parable or simile. Dreams speak to the heart rather than the intellect. That is how they can bring new awareness. Cryptic to the rational intellect, they can slip past the limiting barriers of our intellectual prejudices and reach consciousness where they may have profound effects. For instance, memories, insights, and associations may awaken dormant qualities in the personality. In this way the dream symbols are catalysts of new values and meanings and can bring a rebirth to the psyche.

> Dreams are impartial, spontaneous products of the unconscious psyche, outside the control of the will. They are pure nature; they show us the unvarnished, natural truth, and are therefore fitted, as nothing else is,to give us back an attitude that accords with our basic human nature when our consciousness has strayed too far from its foundations and run into an impasse.[2]

Jung insists that we do not need rational understanding for these modifications to take effect. "Understanding is not an exclusively intellectual process for, as experience shows, a man may be influenced, and indeed convinced in the most effective way, by innumerable things of which he has no intellectual understanding."[3] In most cases, Jung claims, problems which can for a time obsess us are not so much solved as outgrown. Our orientation has changed and old problems no longer hold their intensity. It is not usually intellectual persuasion that changes us; more often what we are responding to are symbolic images. Sometimes the process goes unremarked and we are only aware that new interests claim our attention.

In Dostoyevsky's *The Idiot*, the narrator interprets the function of dreams in a manner very similar to Jung's description.

> You smile at the absurdity of your dream, and at the same time you feel that in the intermingling of those absurdities some idea lies hidden, but an idea that is real, something belonging to your true life, something that exists and has always existed in your heart; it is as though something new and prophetic, something you have been expecting, has been told you in your dream; your impression is very vivid: it may be joyful or agonizing, but what it is and what was said to you—all this you can neither understand nor remember.[4]

In the novels of Dostoyevsky, dreams often appear as the instrument of self-knowledge and transformation, leading to profound inner change or rebirth. Hermann Hesse called Dostoyevsky's ideal of rebirth an "asiatic" idea, and there is evidence to support his contention. In *The Brothers Karamazov*, for instance, Father Zossima, who is a mid-wife of spiritual rebirth, belongs to the "elder" system, which is connected with Eastern esoteric schools.

> Authorities on the subject assert that the institution of "elders" is of recent date, not more than a hundred years old in our monasteries, though in the orthodox East, especially in Sinai and Athos, it has existed over a thousand years. It is maintained that it existed in ancient times in Russia also, but through the calamities which overtook Russia—the Tartars, civil war, the interruption of relations with the East after the destruction of Constantinople—this institution fell into oblivion. It was revived among us towards the end of last century. . . . This institution of elders is not founded on theory, but was established in the East from the practice of a thousand years.[5]

Jung, too, made reference to Eastern thought and spirituality. He saw our Western discovery of psychology as only a beginner's attempt, compared to what is a developed art in the East, where methods of integrating unconscious contents were developed to a much higher degree than in the West. He also thought they were more knowledgeable in their use of archetypal symbols. He was not advocating, however, that we copy their methods. Our task, he claimed, is to develop the "East in us" in terms of our Western heritage and history. "It seems to be quite true that the East is at the bottom of the spiritual change we are passing through today. Only this East is not a Tibetan monastery full of Mahatmas, but in a sense lies within us. It is from the depths of our own psychic life that new spiritual forms will arise. . . ."[6]

The question remains as to what these new spiritual forms might be. According to Jung, our Western ideology has been dominated by Faustian archetypes and extraverted goals and ideals; we have valued heroes who were conquerors, won battles, slew dragons, ruled nations, and exploited nature. What would be the "East in us" to compensate that extraversion? If our "East" is to be found in an unconscious introversion, then we might begin to look for it in the work of our own depth psychologists and visionaries, for instance Dostoyevsky, and Jung himself. In almost all of Dostoyevsky's novels, the scenario involves a dynamic interplay between opposing ideologies. The intellectuals, Ivan Karamazov, Raskolnikov, Stavrogin, and so on, are all isolated, alienated individuals who declare their freedom from worn-out old religious ideals, but who ship-wreck on a slavish obsession with their own compulsions. In *Notes From the Underground*, Dostoyevsky describes this outcome as due to having cut themselves off from their whole human life—what he called "will"—where real freedom is found. Instead, they surrendered to only a limited part, their rational ego desires. The only hope for salvation or escape from their obsessions lay in accepting and enduring the moral suffering that their choice against freedom entailed. Only through suffering can they re-find their true being, one that transcends the narrow boundaries of the intellect. If we look at that scenario from a Jungian point of view, what Dostoyevsky described can be interpreted psychologically as pitfalls on the way to individuation. The goal of individuation is also a spiritual quest, the aim being to integrate and balance opposing sides of the self and to re-center from the narrow ego to a wider Self.

Individuation involves suffering through one's inadequacies and failures and assuming responsibility for them. Is this also a religious quest? Although Jung has often been called a mystic, he cannot justifiably be called religious in any traditional sense; but, in the sense that he was a believer in the reality and value of religious experience and of our need to give expression to religious archetypes—in that sense, he was a religious man. Dostoyevsky, on the other hand, was a staunch supporter of the Russian Orthodox Church; yet, when we look at his novels, we find more emphasis upon subjective religious experience than traditional orthodoxy. For instance, in "The Russian Monk" chapter of *The Brothers Karamazov*, Father Zossima expounds all of Dostoyevsky's most cherished ideals. Yet Father Zossima belongs to the esoteric elder system, which is viewed with suspicion by the more traditional monks of the monastery. Zossima is also portrayed as something of a psychic. He foresees Dmitri's suffering, sees through the posturing of Pavlov Karamazov, and instructs Alyosha to stay close to both his brothers because he foresees that *both* will be implicated in their father's murder. He also tells Alyosha to leave the monastery, that his work belongs in the world. If we look at his prophetic ability as a fine-tuned intuitive function in harmony with the rest of his inner being, we can interpret his character in psychological terms as approaching individuation. Stories of his own youthful transgressions and the transformations following them confirm that assumption.

Religious archetypes, according to Jung, are part of our genetic heritage. They give us meaning and purpose in life and cannot be ignored without damage to the psyche. To Jung, Christ was a modern symbol of individuation. For Dostoyevsky, Christ was the reality behind the kind of spiritual rebirth that he describes in his fiction. But in regard to the dreams that precipitate these transformations, it doesn't matter whether one interprets rebirth in Dostoyevsky's terms, as a religious conversion, or in Jung's terms, as a stage in the individuation process. What is significant is the dynamics of that interplay between dreaming and transformation and the possibilities it opens for future discoveries. It is even possible that, as we become more aware of the part that dreams play in both our sleeping and waking consciousness, we may find our way to that missing and elusive "East in us."

In *The Brothers Karamazov*, the theme of rebirth is conveyed through the Biblical metaphor of a kernel of wheat. "Except a corn of wheat fall into the ground and die, it abideth alone; but if it die, it bringeth forth much fruit." If we look at this metaphor from a Jungian point of view, it suggests confrontation with the shadow, the beginning stage of the individuation process. The shadow is the personal unconscious repository of all the repressed qualities and characteristics we deny in ourselves, along with undeveloped parts of our personality. Confronting the shadow demands courage because it means giving up our illusions about ourselves and taking moral responsibility for our transgressions and failures. If we evade that confrontation, we not only hide from ourselves, but we also distort our relationships with others by projecting our own dark side on them. The end result is that we condemn ourselves to alienation and isolation. This is the "sickness unto death" that Kierkegaard described, which is worse than death, precisely because we cannot die and for which the only cure is faith. The death that frees one in the metaphor is the death of an illusory self. In *The Brothers Karamazov*, Ivan is the kernel of wheat that cannot die. His "brain fever," a state in which he is left at the end of the novel, is a metaphor for the sickness unto death. Ivan cannot accept the moral guilt which he knows is his, because that would mean he must give up his intellectual justification for rebellion against "God's world." The waking dream, or vision, in which he encounters his shadow in the form of a supercilious, seedy-looking devil, traps him in an intolerable situation. His intellectual pride keeps him from accepting the revelations of the seedy devil, who exposes all his most cherished theories as pretentious and dishonest rationalizations. He knows that the devil is only a part of himself, but he refuses to know what he knows. He is in total contradiction. Under the strain of that conflict, he cannot "die" and his fate is inconclusive. Alyosha, watching his struggle, says, "He will either rise up in the light of truth, or . . . he'll perish in hate, revenging on himself and on every one his having served the cause he does not believe in."[7]

Dreams have always been regarded as truth-telling oracles, and, according to Jung, "there is usually a grain of truth in such widely disseminated views." Oracular dreams usually appear when one doesn't know the way out of an impasse. Then, according to Jung, the unconscious begins to function and a dream appears from which we infer that something is pointing the way. What normally may be a compensatory function then becomes a guiding thread leading the person in a new direction. There are two such instances in *The Brothers Karamazov*. One concerns Dmitri, whose intemperate nature has led him to potential disaster. Dmitri is driven by his inner conflicts and impulsive excesses, which culminate in his arrest for the murder of his father. He is innocent of that crime, but the arrest brings him to a new awareness of moral responsibility for all life, something he has, until then, never acknowledged. He arrives at that rebirth of the spirit through a powerful dream as he dozes in the police station where he is being interrogated. In the dream, he is riding in a horse-driven cart during a snowstorm, through a village which had been burnt to the ground. Peasant women are lined up along the road, and he is drawn to one in particular, a thin woman holding a crying baby. The peasants are starving, and the baby is crying from cold and hunger. Dmitri experiences a passion of pity; he wants to cry, to do something for them, so they would no longer weep. "Why?" he keeps asking, "Why are they crying? Why don't they feed the babe?" He awakens with "a new light, as of joy," in his face, as he is flooded with the realization that "we are all responsible for all." With that realization his personal problems pale into insignificance. Later he reaffirms that what really matters is the new spiritual life that has come to him. That new spiritual freedom becomes more important to him than his physical freedom; it opens him to both the absolute worth of his relationship to God and his shared responsibility for all humanity. He tells his brother who visits him in prison:

> Brother, these last two months I've found in myself a new man. A new man has risen up in me. He was hidden in me, but would never have come to the surface if it hadn't been for this blow from heaven. I am afraid! And what do I care if I spend twenty years in the mines, breaking out ore with a hammer? I am not a bit afraid of that—it's something else I am afraid of now: that that new man may leave me. . . . Why was it I dreamed of that "babe" at such a moment? Why is the babe so poor? That was a sign to me at that moment. It's for the babe I'm going. Because we are all responsible for all.[8]

Alyosha, Dmitri's younger brother, also gains new understanding through a dream. Deeply devoted to Father Zossima, his teacher, Alyosha's crisis occurs after Zossima's death, when the miracles expected by the entire monastic community fail to manifest and, instead, an unseemly and premature smell of corruption emanates from his corpse. Alyosha responds to that unexpected event with an uncharacteristic rebellion, unable to accept what he sees as the injustice of that disgrace. While keeping vigil at the coffin, he falls asleep and dreams of the wedding feast in Cana. When he awakens, he is free of rebellion. The dream which freed him did not resolve the problem; it did not explain or justify Zossima's stinking corpse, but the vividness of the dream, with its message that "there is no living without joy," dissipates his anguish. Even more significant, an earlier directive from Zossima is somehow conveyed again through the dream, telling him to throw himself upon the earth and kiss it, to love all men, love everything, to water the earth with his tears, and not to be ashamed of that ecstasy, since it was a gift from God to the elect. At this moment, on awakening from his dream, Alyosha obeys the command of Zossima and something changes in his soul.

> But with every instant he felt clearly and, as it were, tangibly, that something firm and unshakable as that vault of heaven had entered into his soul. It was as though some idea had seized the sovereignty of his mind—and it was for all his life and for ever and ever. He had fallen on the earth a weak boy, but he rose up a resolute champion, and he knew and felt it suddenly at the very moment of his ecstasy. And never, never, all his life long, could Alyosha forget that minute.[9]

After three days Alyosha leaves the monastery and goes out, as Zossima had bidden him, to sojourn in the world.

In *Crime and Punishment*, another rebellious young man is transformed through a dream. Raskolnikov, who committed a murder in order to test whether he was an extraordinary person or just a "louse" like ordinary humanity, cannot bring himself to accept moral guilt, even though such feelings intrude obsessively and throw him into conflict. As a consequence he is isolated, cut off from his own inner life as well as from his family and from Sonia, the young woman who loves him. Recovering from an illness in prison, he has a dream which leaves him open and receptive to feeling and to the love he had so long resisted. The dream symbolically portrays his former nihilism and moral relativism as a deadly microbe devastating humanity; however, the dream ends in hope when a purified elite saves the world by founding a new race and a new life. After that dream, Raskolnikov's former conflicts recede and he experiences a new freedom of spirit. Now able to accept and share the love of Sonia, he no longer cares for anything but to retain this new awareness.

All three of these examples are instances of personal rebirth through dreams that bring a new consciousness and a new direction in life, but there are also transformative dreams which prophesy a new direction for humanity as a whole. Significant religious dreams such as these are what indigenous people call "big dreams." These dreams are the common property of all, even though they may come in response to a personal concern, because that concern is shared by many others.

> How is a man to know whether his dream is a "big" or a "little" one? He knows it by an instinctive feeling of significance. He feels so overwhelmed by the impression it makes that he would never think of keeping the dream to himself. He *has* to tell it, on the psychologically correct assumption that it is of general significance.[10]

Prophetic dreams fulfill what Jung called a prospective function. In these dreams there is an anticipation of future conscious achievement, a sort of plan roughed out in advance. These dreams are not, in the strict sense, prophetic. They are really only an anticipation of probabilities which may coincide with the way things happen (but do not have to agree in every detail). A prophetic dream of this sort, whether personal or collective, results from the fusion of subliminal elements. It combines perceptions, thoughts, and feelings which consciousness has not registered because they are only weakly accented. In Dostoyevsky's novels there are several "big dreams" which foresee humanity turning toward an ideal of universal brotherhood. Dostoyevsky saw contemporary life as characterized by a dangerous over-intellectualization at the expense of the heart and the spirit. The price of that imbalance was what he described as a period of isolated individualism. The protagonist in *Notes from the Underground*, an alienated individual, is the product of a society where logic and rationality are valued over feeling and intuition. Since it is in the heart and spirit that moral knowledge resides, when the intellect takes precedence over feeling and intuition the result is moral chaos. Bitter and self-destructive, the underground man is an example of what happens to people in a society that has forgotten its spiritual roots in a shared humanity. Raskolnikov, mentioned above, is another example of misguided intellectualism, as is Ivan in *The Brothers Karamazov*.

Jung held a similar view:

> In our time, it's the intellect that is making darkness, because we've let it take too big a place. Consciousness discriminates, judges, analyzes, and emphasizes the contradictions. It's necessary work up to a point. But analysis kills and synthesis brings to life. We must find out how to get everything back into connection with everything else. We must resist the vice of intellectualism, and get it understood that we cannot only understand.[11]

Because dreams provide an indirect and non-intellectual message through symbolic images, they can address the problem of social isolation without provoking conscious resistance. Prophetic dreams concerning the evolutionary potential of humanity to reach a universal love for all living beings and for the earth appear in *The Brothers Karamazov* and *A Raw Youth*. In both novels Dostoyevsky suggests that a new age for humanity may be dawning once we find our way out of the nihilism and individualism that now dominate us. In *A Raw Youth*, Versilov, one of the protagonists, describes a dream of a previous Golden Age where people lived happy and innocent lives filled with simple-hearted joy and love. That lost paradise becomes a powerful ideal.

> The Golden Age is the most unlikely of all the dreams that have been, but for it men have given up their life and all their strength, for the sake of it prophets have died and been slain, without it the peoples will not live and cannot die, and the feeling of all this I lived through, as it were, in that dream.[12]

Jung explains the archetypal significance of a Golden Age as an idea produced by the unconscious, which returns to us in dreams, compensating for the complexity of modern life.

> The world had become impoverished in beauty, and people harked back to the Romans, to their nature-bound thinking, reminding themselves of those distant ages when every bush harbored a shrine, when those most marvelous figures of fantasy, the gods, were nothing other than perfect human beings. After this epoch, the Renaissance, they began remembering the ancient Greeks, Rousseau preached the return to Nature, and the classicists . . . the return to the sun of Homer. And in our century we want to go still further back into the past, in our hounded age there rise up before our wistful eyes epochs when man communed with clouds and sun, wind and tempest, the Golden Age of humanity, as it is still sporadically reflected in the primitive, becoming more radiant the further we climb exploringly the genealogical tree of the present races, back to the ancient Egyptians and Babylonians, to the Biblical tribes and their forebears. . . . We all long to go home to the joys of the Golden Age, which let us be natural, graceful, and conscious of our strength, delivered from the bane of our time, the neuroses.[13]

On awakening from his dream, Versilov is filled with the love of all humanity; but a vision follows that dream, which he describes as the "last day of civilization," a melancholy moment of truth, when humanity was forced to recognize the death of God. His final vision, however, is one of redemption, when all the love and passion that formerly was directed to God is turned upon all life.

> All the wealth of love lavished of old upon Him, who was immortal, would be turned upon the whole of Nature, on the world, on men, on every blade of grass. They would inevitably grow to love the earth and life as they gradually became aware of their own transitory and finite nature, and with a special love, not as of old, they would begin to observe and would discover in Nature phenomena and secrets which they had not suspected before, for they would look on Nature with new eyes, as a lover looking on his beloved.[14]

Only after that transition, when humanity has conquered its inhumanity to man through a compassion for all life, does God return. Then humanity is reborn. Versilov admits that all this is "a fantasy and a most improbable one."

In *The Brothers Karamazov*, Father Zossima speaks with a mysterious visitor who has a vision of a rebirth of the human spirit. In this new world, as in the transformed humanity of Versilov's vision, "all are responsible for all." But first, the visitor claims, we must endure the period of isolation which precedes the new age.

> Why, the isolation that prevails everywhere, above all in our age—it has not fully developed, it has not reached its limit yet. For every one strives to keep his individuality as apart as possible, wishes to secure the greatest possible fullness of life for himself; but meantime all his efforts result not in attaining fullness of life, but self-destruction, for instead of self-realization he ends by arriving at complete solitude. All mankind in our age have split up into units, they all keep apart, each in his own groove, each one holds aloof, hides himself and hides what he has, from the rest, and he ends by being repelled by others and repelling them. . . . For he is accustomed to rely upon himself alone and to cut himself off from the whole; he has trained himself not to believe in the help of others, in men and inhumanity, and only trembles for fear he should lose his money and the privileges that he has won for himself.[15]

The visitor commends Zossima for his preaching that we are all responsible to all for all, but Zossima, who was then a young man, expresses his doubt that humanity will ever achieve that understanding, even though it was what he preached. "Is not it simply a dream of ours?" he asks. But the mysterious visitor reassures him that it can come about in reality.

> Believe me, this dream, as you call it, will come to pass without doubt; it will come, but not now, for every process has its law. It's a spiritual, psychological process. To transform the world, to recreate it afresh, men must turn into another path psychologically. Until you have become really in actual fact, a brother to everyone, brotherhood will not come to pass. No sort of scientific teaching, no kind of common interest, will ever teach men to share property and privileges with equal consideration for all. Every one will think his share too small and they will be always envying, complaining and attacking one another. You ask when it will come to pass; it will come to pass, but first we have to go through the period of isolation.[16]

In "The Meaning of Psychology for Modern Man," Jung describes contemporary life as one of dissociation, although he also describes it as a climax, heralding "the throes of birth." He sees our time as similar to the dissociation of the Roman Empire, which was simultaneously an age of rebirth. And in *The Undiscovered Self*, Jung comes to a conclusion similar to that of the mysterious visitor—though not quite as optimistic:

> The effect on *all* individuals, which one would like to see realized, may not set in for hundreds of years, for the spiritual transformation of mankind follows the slow tread of the centuries and cannot be hurried or held up by any rational process of reflection, let alone brought to fruition in one generation. What does lie within our reach, however, is the change in individuals who have, or create for themselves, an opportunity to influence others of like mind.[17]

For the same reasons as Jung, Dostoyevsky, too, believed that real change in human society could only come about through the psychological change that begins in individuals and spreads from person to person. That is the message in the epilogue of *The Brothers Karamazov*, where Alyosha begins to fill his task of bringing Zossima's teaching to the world, and especially to the youth, whom he convinces of the power of love and universal brotherhood. Even if one has to do it alone, Zossima taught, and one's conduct seems to be crazy, one must set an example and draw men's souls out of their solitude, spur them on to some act of brotherly love, so the great idea may not die. One of the metaphors Zossima uses to express the common tie between all living beings is that humanity is like an ocean—"all is flowing and blending; a touch in one place sets up movement at the other end of the earth." His command to Alyosha to "love the earth, birds, animals, trees" is an expression of this connectedness.

> Love all God's creation, the whole and every grain of sand in it. Love every leaf, every ray of God's light. Love the animals, love the plants, love everything. If you love everything, you will perceive the divine mystery in things. Once you perceive it, you will begin to comprehend it better every day.... Brothers, love is a teacher; but one must know how to acquire it, for it is hard to acquire, it is dearly bought, it is won slowly by long labour.[18]

Here, as in Versilov's vision, humanity only becomes transformed when universal love becomes a reality. Versilov's vision culminates in the reappearance of God, but Zossima is less orthodox and more mystical. "Much on earth is hidden from us, but to make up for that we have been given a precious mystic sense of our living bond with the other world, with the higher heavenly world and the roots of our thoughts and feelings are not here but in other worlds."[19]

The secret behind the dreams and visions of both Versilov and Zossima is that universal love alters one's consciousness, and new understanding comes with that expansion of awareness. Zossima's visitor claimed that when responsible caring for everything permeated human consciousness, then the "law" of psychological transformation would bring about a rebirth of humanity to a new understanding of universal brotherhood. If dreams can open that door to the capacity to love, then the dream becomes a genuine source of transformation. According to Jung, it is in the deep unconscious that we are at one with all humanity, for we share the same archetypal inheritance, and he, too, claimed that we were at the threshold of a new spiritual epoch, that modern man, fascinated by his own unconscious, was searching within himself for the replacement for a missing God and for the affective bonds that can reunite all humanity. In this quest, both Dostoyevsky and Jung see the dream as offering that regenerative force.

> The dream is a little hidden door in the innermost and most secret recesses of the soul, opening into that cosmic night which was psyche long before there was any ego-consciousness, and which will remain psyche no matter how far our ego-consciousness extends. For all ego-consciousness is isolated; because it separates and discriminates, it knows only particulars, and it sees only those that can be related to the ego. Its essence is limitation, even though it reach to the farthest nebulae among the stars. All consciousness separates; but in dreams we put on the likeness of that more universal, truer, more eternal man dwelling in the darkness of primordial night. There he is still the whole, and the whole is in him, indistinguishable from nature and bare of all egohood. It is from these all-uniting depths that the dream arises.[20]

Notes

1. Carl Gustav Jung, *Collected Works* vol. 10, trans. R. F. C. Hull (Princeton: Princeton University Press, 1975), 149.

2. Jung, *Collected Works*, 149.

3. Carl Gustav Jung, *Dreams*, trans. R. F. C. Hull (Princeton: Princeton University Press, 1974), 30-31.

4. Fyodor Dostoyevsky, *The Idiot*, trans. David Magarshack (London: Penguin Classics, 1955), 492.

5. Fyodor Dostoyevsky, *The Brothers Karamazov*, trans. Constance Garnett (New York: Modern Library, 1950), 26-27.

6. Carl Gustav Jung, *Modern Man in Search of a Soul*, trans. Delland Baynes (New York: Harvest Book, Harcourt Brace and World, 1933), 217.

7. Dostoyevsky, *The Brothers Karamazov*, 796.

8. Dostoyevsky, *The Brothers Karamazov, 719-20.*

9. Dostoyevsky, *The Brothers Karamazov,* 437.

10. Carl Gustav Jung, *Two Essays on Analytical Psychology*, trans. R. F. C. Hull (Cleveland: World Publishing, 1967), 188.

11. Carl Gustav Jung, *C. G. Jung Speaking*, eds. William McGuire and R. F. C. Hull (Princeton: Princeton University Press, 1977), 420.
12. Fyodor Dostoyevsky, *A Raw Youth*, trans. Constance Garnett (New York: Dial Press, 1947), 508.
13. Jung, *C. G. Jung Speaking*, 43-44.
14. Dostoyevsky, *A Raw Youth*, 513.
15. Dostoyevsky, *The Brothers Karamazov,* 363.
16. Dostoyevsky, *The Brothers Karamazov,* 362-63.
17. Jung, *Collected Works*, 302-3.
18. Dostoyevsky, *The Brothers Karamazov,* 382-83.
19. Dostoyevsky, *The Brothers Karamazov,* 382-83.
20. Jung, *Collected Works*, 144-45.

CHAPTER SEVEN

Where Angels Dare to Tread

Wings of Desire

> What if there were a living agency beyond our everyday human world—something even more purposeful than electrons? Do we delude ourselves in thinking that we possess and control our own psyches, and is what science calls the "psyche" not just a question-mark arbitrarily confined within the skull, but rather a door that opens upon the human world from a world beyond, allowing unknown and mysterious powers to act upon man and carry him on the wings of the night to a more than personal destiny?[1]
>
> C. G. Jung

In the opening scene of *Wings of Desire* a hand slowly writes the following words, accompanied by the recitation of an over-voice:

When the child was a child
It walked with its arms swinging.
It wanted the stream to be a river,
The river a torrent,
And this puddle to be the sea.
When the child was a child
It didn't know it was a child.
Everything was full of life,
And all life was one.
When the child was a child

> It had no opinions about anything.
> It had no habits.
> It sat cross-legged, took off running,
> Had a cowlick in its hair,
> And didn't make a face when photographed.[2]

The innocence and wonderment of childhood, expressed in this opening scene, is repeated at intervals throughout the film, linking together with its symbolism what might otherwise be viewed as disjointed episodes. Along with evoking the naive optimism of childhood, these recitations, like a Greek chorus, are a reminder of everyone's childhood questions—the ones that have faded, unanswered, into the forgotten past where we banish all "childish things."

> When the child was a child that was the time of these questions.
> Why am I me, and not you?
> Why am I here, and why not there?
> When did time begin, and where does space end?
> Isn't life under the sun just a dream?

Immediately following the opening recitation, we skim over the rooftops of Berlin and pause with the startling appearance of an unlikely angel atop a tall tower, who placidly observes the milling crowds below. No harp or flowing white gown signals his presence as an angel. He appears as an ordinary middle-aged man in a dark overcoat. Only his casual stance on the edge of the tower together with a pair of briefly appearing and quickly fading large transparent wings betray his identity, which is soon confirmed when we realize that we are hearing, through his telepathic consciousness, the thoughts of all the people among whom he later passes or lingers, invisible to them all, with the exception now and then of a child, whose spiritual perception is not yet extinguished by the weight of flesh.

It is only gradually that we become aware, through the intervals between a panoramic scanning of the city, of a love story developing between the angel, Damiel, and the beautiful trapeze artist, Marion. Preceding that story, however, we follow the activities of the two angels, Damiel and Cassiel, who carry on their eternal work of witnessing and recording events significant to them but inexplicable to us—unique moments and incidents selected at apparently temporal random from the lives of earthbound humanity.

> Cassiel — 20 years ago today a Soviet jet fighter crashed into the lake at Spandau. Fifty years ago there were . . .
> Damiel — The Olympic games.

Cassiel — 200 years ago, Blanchard flew over the city in a balloon. ...And today... on the Lilienthaler Chaussee, a man, walking, slowed down and looked over his shoulder into space...
Damiel — A woman on the street folded her umbrella while it rained... and let herself get drenched.

As we, the audience, in turn witness the lives of the angels, we discover a parallel to our human "divine discontent" in the "experiential envy" of the angels, who are confined to a bloodless black and white dimension of the spirit; and we witness their longing to break out of their spiritual limitations and to encounter, sense, feel the weight of physical existence. Damiel, especially, yearns to know, not just observe, physical life, and his desire intensifies when he falls in love with the beautiful Marion. His yearning for experience finally culminates in a "leap of life"—a reversal of the Kierkegaardian leap of faith; this leap is a descent into mortality, time, the senses, and physical love. There are many implications for collective human life in this descent of the divine and union with the human.

Subplots intrude repeatedly into the story of Damiel and Marion—some only fragments, an interlude here and there, some more sustained; but all of them contribute to the theme of the interaction of human and angel, suggesting a collective significance along with the particular history of this unique union. The most prominent subplot concerns the role of Homer, the aged storyteller, who is accompanied by an attentive Cassiel. Another subplot revolves around an earlier immigrant angel, Peter Falk, who tries to facilitate the migration of angels to the world of human experience. At the end, when the incarnated Damiel merges his life with Marion, the meaning of this integration between human and angel becomes more apparent, especially in its significance for the question of human evolution. The predominant image of childhood as an appropriate symbol becomes meaningful at this point.

The descent of Damiel and his union with Marion can be approached through a Jungian perspective in two ways; the most obvious is the union of these lovers as a symbolic expression of individuation both for that unique pair and for the human species as a whole. Spirit and matter unite in a holy marriage to bring integration and completion where there had been separation, unconsciousness, and longing. The second approach is less obvious; it is suggested by Jung's treatment of the *Book of Job*, drawing upon his interpretation of divine incarnation and contributing to that myth of meaning. Marion and Damiel are two beings in search of their own wholeness, and their eventual merger symbolizes the creation of a new image for humanity.

In an interview in 1934, Jung addressed the problem of our age as a spiritual or religious problem:

> Man today hungers and thirsts for a safe relationship to the psychic forces within himself. His consciousness, recoiling from the difficulties of the modern world, lacks a relationship to safe spiritual conditions. This makes him neurotic, ill, frightened. Science has told him that there is no God, and that matter is all there is. This has deprived humanity of its blossom, its feeling of well-being and of safety in a safe world.[3]

In the scenes where the camera scans the city, we pick up, through the angel's consciousness, fragments of that anxiety-ridden humanity. In an early scene a woman on a bicycle mutters to herself: "At last mad, at last no longer alone! At last mad, at last redeemed! At last insane, at last at peace." From another, a tired old woman on the subway: "When will you finally pray with your own words . . . and not for eternal life? Traitors . . . deserters . . . you think I don't know who you are?" From yet another anxious inner voice on the subway: "In any case, all that is crap. Why am I living, in fact? Why am I living? . . . Why am I living?"

Marion, too, struggles for meaning and self-knowledge. After learning that the circus will close prematurely for lack of funds, Marion walks out of the tent and sits alone, deep in thought.

> All those I've known . . . who remain, and who will remain in my head. It begins, it always ends. It was too good. At last, outside in the city, I'll find out who I am, who I've become. . . . As a child, I wanted to live on an island. A woman alone, gloriously alone. That's it. Emptied, incompatible. Fear, the fear, the fear . . . The look of a small animal lost in the wood. Who are you? I don't know anymore . . . Emptiness . . . Emptiness.

Later, in her trailer, she confronts her fear and struggles again for self-knowledge. "I'd like to know. I know nothing. I'm a little afraid." Asleep, Marion dreams of Damiel, who appears winged and in armor, as her lover. That dream leaves her with a feeling of anticipation. When, the next morning, she says good-bye to the circus crew, she is lighthearted. Some dreams, according to Jung, are precognitive in that the unconscious is aware of the progress of events which have been unfolding but which have not yet reached the level of consciousness. Even though that knowledge may not be accessible to consciousness, yet one's mood is affected by that awareness. Marion's dream has alerted her unconsciously to a premonition of her future meeting with Damiel. Her farewell to the crew is a joyful reflection of her inner lightness and optimism. We hear her inner thoughts: "I couldn't say who I am, I haven't the slightest idea. I'm someone who has no roots, no story, no country. And I like it that way. I'm here, I'm free, and I can imagine anything." When Cassiel joins her, though invisible, his presence adds to her anticipation. "Everything is possible. I only need to raise my eyes and once again, I become the world. Now, in this very place, a feeling of happiness that I could have forever." Since, according to Jung, the unconscious is not limited by time and space, Marion's anticipation is accountable. ". . . we have irrefutable evidence that at least parts of our psyche are not subject to the laws of space and time, otherwise perceptions outside space and time would be altogether impossible—yet they exist, they happen. All cases of telepathic clairvoyance, predictions of the future—they exist."[4]

That evening when Marion encounters Peter Falk and he asks if she is looking for somebody, she answers, "I don't know, I just want to find someone."

Marion is the beautiful trapeze artist who dreams of Damiel, but she is also symbolic of all humanity, searching for outer love and inner completion. Her attempt to escape the pull of earth by flying "like an angel" on the trapeze is the outer expression of her struggle for an inner connection with spirit. The crew call her an angel, but she knows that what she is seeking still eludes her. She complains to them that she cannot fly with those "chicken wings," the circus trappings imposed upon her. In fact, the wings are incongruous and childish looking, detracting from the flawless grace of her movements on the trapeze. A chicken does not soar in the air. Marion is right to object to them.

The closure of the circus threatens to destroy her dream of a career as a trapeze artist; but, as an inner threat, it means she may have to remain earthbound, fail in the search for her own individuation. Her constant question, "Who am I?" is the groping for her own unconscious spiritual identity, which she reaches only in her dream of union with the lover-angel. The actual meeting with Damiel, foreshadowed by the dream, is transformative and opens her to her own inner depths so that the physical union is simultaneously an inner expansion of consciousness and self-awareness as well as a recognition of him as the one for whom she had been yearning.

The longing of Marion for her own spiritual identity, although symbolically significant for all moderns, may not be a pursuit widely acknowledged as such and may only betray its presence in the anxiety and denial of spirit so prevalent in our time. Yet, even those who deny the reality of spirit, or acknowledge it only as myth or fantasy, are at least familiar with it as such. An angel's longing for a descent into matter, however, is a startling reversal; an angel who wants to be human upsets our ordinary assumptions. Seeing ourselves through an angel's eyes as objects of envy is a new perspective. Damiel complains to Cassiel: "It's great to live only by the spirit, to testify day by day for eternity only to the spiritual side of people. But sometimes I get fed up with my spiritual existence. Instead of forever hovering above I'd like to feel there's some weight to me . . . to end my eternity and bind me to earth." Damiel wants to be able to say "now" instead of "since always," and "forever"—to suspect, instead of forever *knowing* all, "to be able to say 'ah' and 'oh' and 'hey' instead of 'yes' and 'amen.'" Cassiel agrees with Damiel and adds to this litany: "To do no more than observe, collect, testify, preserve! To remain a spirit. Keep your distance! Keep your word!"

We are accustomed to see angels as guardians, watching over and caring for humanity. We are not accustomed to think of angels as discontented. But Damiel is an angel with needs. He needs life. Jung comments precisely on that need: "There are many spirits, both light and dark. We should, therefore, be prepared to accept the view that spirit is not absolute, but something relative that needs completing and perfecting through life."[5] "Life," Jung says, "is a touchstone for the truth of the spirit. . . . Life and spirit are two powers or necessities between which man is placed. Spirit gives meaning to his life, and the possibility of its greatest development. But life is essential to spirit, since its truth is nothing if it cannot live."[6] Man is distinct from the angels, Jung claims, because he can receive revelations, be disobedient, grow, and change. It is that limitation on him that haunts Damiel, who wants to do more than pretend to be participating in life. Knowing all of spiritual life and enduring in eternity, he is nevertheless deprived because he knows nothing about the physical, material existence of those whose lives he records in his notebooks. He is an outsider, pressing his nose against a spiritual barrier and unable to know what coffee tastes like, what red looks like, what it is like "to feel your skeleton moving along as you walk," what it means to know you are mortal. He remains forever incomplete in his eternity without that knowledge.

When he watches the acrobatic act of Marion in the circus tent, his already "unangelic" act of falling in love with her is the catalyst which leads to his leap into life.

In the library scene, angels perch on balconies, lean over banisters, and wander among the readers, old and young, while rich choral music is heard, giving the library the atmosphere of a cathedral. Hovering over the shoulders of the readers, the angels bring encouragement and comfort. On the whole, however, the effect of the angels on the people they linger with or accompany is ambiguous. Sometimes their presence has a catalytic effect; for example, the response of a despondent man on the subway who, before Damiel approaches him, is mired in his depressive thoughts. "You're lost, but it might last a long time. Disowned by your parents, betrayed by your wife . . . your friend's in another town. Your children only remember your speech defect. You feel like slapping yourself when you look in the mirror." When Damiel sits beside him and puts his arm on the man's shoulders, there is an instant reaction. "What's that? Something's happening! I'm still here! If I want it, if only I want it . . . I have to want it, then I can get out of it again. I got myself into it. I'll drag myself out again. And why not? Mama was right, 'Don't let yourself get so upset like that.'" When Damiel comes upon a man dying in the street from the effects of a motorcycle accident, he stays with him, leading the man's thoughts to the recall of events, places, and people in his life, and so to a peaceful death. At other times, however, the angels seem unable to make their influence felt and remain helpless.

In the same scene, one of the readers, whose voice we hear, is reading a passage which describes the angel Cassiel. The reading is a verbatim account of a passage from Gustav Davidson's *Dictionary of Angels*.

> *Cassiel* (Casiel, Casziel, Kafziel)—the angel of solitudes and tears who "shews forth the unity of the eternal kingdom." Cassiel is one of the rulers of the planet Saturn, also a ruling prince of the 7th Heaven and one of the *sarim* (princes) of the order of powers. Sometimes he appears as the angel of temperance.[7]

No similar reference to Damiel is made in that scene, but the Davidson book has the following description of him: "Damiel—angel of the 5th hour, serving under the rulership of Sazquiel; or angel of the 9th hour, serving under the rulership of Vadriel. Damiel is invoked in the conjuration of the Sword."[8] In that same book we are told that angels perform a multiplicity of duties and tasks, but that preeminently they serve God by ceaseless chanting of glorias while they circle the throne. But they also carry out missions from God to man. ". . . many serve man directly as guardians, counselors, guides, judges, interpreters, cooks, comforters, dragomen, matchmakers, and gravediggers."[9] In the Epilogue of the *Dictionary of Angels*, a group of angels is described as "Watchers":

> The Watchers are the sons of God (Genesis 6) sent from heaven to instruct the children of men; they fell after they descended to earth and cohabited with the daughters of men—for which act they were condemned (so legend reports) and became fallen angels. But not all Watchers descended: those that remained are the holy Watchers, and they reside in the 5th Heaven. The evil Watchers dwell either in the 3rd Heaven or in Hell.[10]

It is tempting to interpret Damiel as an angel who descended and Cassiel as a Watcher who remained; however, Cassiel is ruler of the 7th Heaven and Damiel, although he descended and cohabited with a daughter of men, is not included among the fallen angels. The term "Watcher" does seem appropriate though, even if the interpretation doesn't quite fit.

Why Cassiel's description appears in the film script remains a question. Perhaps it is there as an explanation for the gravity of his character, which has none of the intensity and enthusiasm of Damiel. Cassiel's care-worn face suggests a history of spiritual suffering and he pursues his task of witnessing with the patient endurance of one who shoulders heavy burdens. Hovering beside a young man rejected in love who is about to commit suicide by jumping from the roof of a building, Cassiel attempts to deter him. Although he sits beside him and embraces him, the young man fails to respond. When he leaps to his death, Cassiel, his face a grimace of pain, cries out in anguish.

Thus we know very little of the meaning behind the presence of the angels in this film. Their main function seems to be to witness and take note of human activity. Sometimes they can be effective in guiding the thoughts of people, and other times they are helpless. They can be long-suffering and patiently endure their eternity as witness, or they can renounce that obligation through free choice and leap into the weight of material existence, as does Damiel.

There is even a suggestion of a reciprocity between angel and man; for instance, the suffering of the young suicide creates emotional pain in Cassiel. More puzzling is the claim that the angels learned to talk from their observation of the development of human speech. In that digression on the evolution of life on earth we learn nothing about any cosmic purpose for the universe or for humanity, or for the presence of the angels themselves. However, a sense of some underlying matrix of meaning haunts that scene, as it does the film as a whole.

The scene in question occurs after Damiel has led Cassiel to the circus tent to observe the children's matinee, followed by the over-voice of Damiel reflecting again on "when the child was a child . . .," contrasting the innocence of childhood with the disillusionment of adulthood. "It had a precise picture of paradise and now it can only guess at it. It could not conceive of Nothingness and today it shudders at the idea."

Damiel and Cassiel remind each other of their first visit to the Valley of the Primeval River, when "history had not yet begun." They describe the melting of a glacier, then the myriad of years during which there came fish, bees, flies, and finally wild cats, buffalo, and so on. They recall, too, the emergence of the human animal: "Do you remember how, one morning out of the savanna—its forehead smeared with grass—the biped appeared, our long-awaited image, and its first work was a shout: was it 'ach' or 'ah' or 'oh,' or was it merely a groan?" At this point Cassiel adds the provocative comment that the angels, in whose image the human was created, learn speech and laughter from this material copy of themselves. "At last we were able to laugh for the first time. And through this man's shout and the calls of his successor, we learned to speak." This strange reciprocity between human and angel permeates the whole film, suggesting that both need each other for their own growth and development. Angels yearn for the reality of the senses while humans grope for spirit which is trapped in the heaviness of matter. One implication of the evolutionary interlude is precisely this vision of an evolution in process where the forces of matter and spirit strain toward a union that has slowly, through eons, been moving toward that goal. The final scenes of the movie point precisely to that end.

As Damiel recounts the beginning of war and aggression—continuing to this day—Cassiel reminds him that the first story of joyful growth is also still going on. But Damiel is impatient with that slow progress and announces his intention to join history in an active role.

> Yes! To conquer a history for myself! I want to turn what I've learned from my timeless downward-watching into sustaining a hasty glance, a short shout, an acrid smell. I've been outside long enough. Absent, long enough. Out of the world long enough! I'll enter into the history of the world!

Shortly thereafter the deed is done, and Damiel awakens to a world of color. The world seen through an angel's eyes is black and white. Awakening as a human, Damiel finds himself surrounded by colors. The breast armor which falls and strikes his head acquaints him with the taste of blood and the color red. He begins to identify the colors. "I'm beginning to understand!" Damiel's new-born childish delight and excitement in rubbing his hands together, in drinking coffee, in walking briskly, is articulated again through the child imagery. "When the child was a child apples and bread were enough for him. And it is still that way. . . . It reached for the cherries in the treetop with the elation it still feels today."

The mystery of Peter Falk's intuitive apprehension of Damiel while an angel is clarified for him when he later encounters him as a fellow human. Damiel is astonished to hear that Peter Falk is also a former angel who chose incarnation, and that "there's lots of us." Peter Falk, who recognizes the presence of angels although he can no longer see them, plays the part of a psychopomp, encouraging other angels to cross the threshold into what had been for them an area of unconsciousness—the life of the senses. He refuses to tell Damiel about physical life, saying, "You have to find out yourself, that's the fun of it!" He recognizes the presence of Cassiel, as he did Damiel's, and greets him, too, as "Campañero," confiding that he has "so many things to tell him."

The admission that there are many incarnated angels places the love story of Marion and Damiel in a new context, one where not only collective humanity but the whole angelic realm are engaged in a movement toward new beginnings—toward a rebirth, a new kind of life, a new childhood for human and angel alike.

The possibility of a new beginning for humanity through a transformation of consciousness appears repeatedly in the writing of Jung.

> We don't know our unconscious personality. We have hints, we have certain ideas, but we don't know it really. Nobody can say where man ends. That is the beauty of it, you know; it's very interesting. The unconscious of man can reach God knows where. There we are going to make discoveries.[11]

In defending his reference to changes related to the Zodiac, Jung says:

> It's a matter of experience that the symbolism changes from one sign to another, and there is the risk that this passage will be all the more difficult for the men of today and tomorrow because they no longer believe in it, no longer want to be conscious of it. Why, when Pope Pius XII in one of his last discourses deplored that the world was no longer conscious enough of the presence of angels, he was saying to his faithful Catholics in Christian terms exactly what I am trying to say in terms of psychology to those who stand more chance of understanding this language than any other.[12]

"A lot will still have to happen to mankind," Jung writes, "many things will have to change before the new style comes to birth, the new formula for the realization of humanity."[13]

Marion and Damiel, when they finally meet as man and woman, are cognizant of the role they play in that new birth. Their meeting is in the bar of a large, dimly-lit night club. The night club could be a parody of contemporary society; crowds of people stand together in physical proximity and spiritual isolation, listening to the wailing voice of the lead singer of a contemporary band. Cassiel, who also appears among them, turns from the depressing scene and leans his forehead against the wall. At the bar, where Damiel sits, the atmosphere is lighter. When Marion approaches and takes a seat beside him, they need no introduction. Marion is instantly transformed by his presence and begins to speak with a new understanding.

> It's time to get serious. I was often alone, but I never lived alone. When I was with someone, I was often happy, but I also felt it's all a matter of chance. These people were my parents, but it could have been others. Why was that brown-eyed boy my brother, and why not the green-eyed boy on the opposite platform? The taxi driver's daughter was my friend, but I could just as well have embraced a horse's head. I was with a man, I was in love, but I could just as well have left him there, and continued on with the stranger who came

toward us. Look at me, or don't. Give me your hand, or don't. No, don't give me your hand, and look the other way . . . I never played with anyone, and yet I've never opened my eyes and thought: 'This is it. It's finally getting serious.' So I've grown older. Was I the only one who wasn't serious? Is it our times that are not serious? I was never lonely, neither when I was alone, nor with others. I would have liked to be alone at last. Loneliness means: at last I am whole. Now I can say it, because today I am finally lonely.

Encountering her own completion, Marion also experiences a moment of truth—that from now on her life will be different. "Life that just happens in and for itself is not real life," says Jung; "it is real only when it is *known*. Only a unified personality can experience life, not that personality which is split up into partial aspects."[14]

The presence of Damiel acts as a transformative agent, evoking in Marion a realization that her past had been characterized by a lack of serious commitment; never conscious of her own identity—her Self, her own uniqueness, she was never conscious of being lonely. One man was interchangeable with another. But now, united with her own spirituality, she is aware of herself as whole; she can no longer drift with chance.

> No more coincidence! The new moon of decision! I don't know if destiny exists. But decision does exist. Decide! Now, WE are the times. Not only the whole city, but the whole world is taking part in our decision. We two are more than just two. We personify something. We are sitting in the people's plaza and the whole plaza is filled with people, who all wish for what we wish for. We are deciding everyone's game! . . . There's no story greater than ours, that of man and woman. It will be a story of giants, invisible, transposable, a story of new ancestors. Look, my eyes! They are the picture of necessity, of the future of everyone on the plaza.

The next morning Damiel seals the commitment both to Marion and to the creative birth they have consummated. We hear his inner voice:

> Something has happened, it is still happening. It is binding! . . . No mortal child was created, but an immortal common image . . . The image we created will be with me when I die. I will have lived within it. Only the amazement about the two of us—the amazement about man and woman—only that made a human being of me. I . . . know . . . now . . . what . . . no . . . angel . . . knows. (The last sentence is handwritten on the screen.)

Damiel, the angel who values the life of the senses, suggests a new vision of humanity, but Jung had already, in *The Spiritual Problem of Modern Man*, predicted this development when he claimed that the characteristic symptoms of our time show how the ideal of humanism is made to embrace the body. "The attractive power of the psyche brings about a new self-estimation—a re-estimation of the basic facts of human nature. We can hardly be surprised if this leads to the rediscovery of the body after its long depreciation in the name of the spirit."[15]

According to Jung, the body lays claim to equal recognition and, like the psyche, it, too, exerts a fascination; there is no longer an antithesis between mind and matter.

> But if we can reconcile ourselves with the mysterious truth that spirit is the living body seen from within, and the body the outer manifestation of the living spirit—the two being really one—then we can understand why it is that the attempt to transcend the present level of consciousness must give its due to the body.[16]

Damiel and Marion find precisely this reconciliation for themselves and for the future of humanity.

In our last view of Damiel and Marion, he is stabilizing the rope upon which she climbs to practice her acrobatics. He, incarnate spirit, feet planted firmly on the ground, holds fast the rope on which Marion, child of the earth, soars and turns in the air.

Jung, in his anticipation of a new beginning for humanity, may not have foreseen a merging of angel and human, but he did describe a separation of spirit and matter as the problem of our time, and he saw the resolution of that problem as one that would have to be solved through the action of individuals.

> What is a problem of the present day? If we speak of a general problem nowadays, it is because it exists in the heads of many people. These individuals are somehow chosen by fate and destined by their own natures to suffer under a collectively unsatisfactory condition and to make it a problem. Therefore it is always single individuals who are moved by the collective problem and who are called upon to respond and contribute to its solution by tackling it in their own lives and not running away from it.[17]

Thus, one can look upon the union of Damiel and Marion as symbolic of the individuation process itself, and equally as symbolic of the individuation of humankind.

Reference to that new beginning for humanity, through the poetic interludes of the life of the child, is in Damiel's voice, but the author of the child stories could well be Homer, the aged storyteller, who warns that the storyteller's significance and fate have become precarious in our time. Throughout the ages, he tells us, the storyteller has revealed every man. As he passes Damiel on the library stairs, the storyteller also reveals his own thoughts:

> With time, my listeners became my readers. They no longer sit in a circle. . . . Instead they sit apart . . . and one knows nothing about the other. I am an old man with a broken voice. But the story still rises from deep down and the half-open mouth repeats . . . with strength and clarity, a liturgy for which no one need be initiated to the meaning of the words and phrases.

With a solicitous Cassiel beside him in the library, we hear Homer's thoughts:

> The world seems to be sinking into dusk, but I tell the stories as in the beginning, in my sing-song voice, which sustains me, saved by the tale from the troubling present, and protected for the future. It is finished, the great breadth of the old days, no more going back and forth over the centuries. Now I can only think from day to day.

As documentary films of World War II flash before us on the screen, Homer laments the fact that no one has succeeded in singing an epic about peace. He asks himself, "What is it about peace, that keeps its inspiration from enduring and makes it almost untellable?" His heroes, Homer says, are no longer the warriors and kings, but the things of peace.

In a comment on his film, the director, Wim Wenders, describes his heroes. "The heroes of my story are angels. Yes, angels. And why not? We are accustomed to see so many monsters and imaginary creatures in the cinema. Well, why not some beneficent spirits for a change?"[18] But beneficent heroes are possible only if the storyteller endures, and with him the preservation of childhood. "If humanity loses its story-teller," says Homer, "it loses at the same time its childhood." That danger haunts Homer who describes "the immortal singer" who, abandoned by his mortal listeners, lost his voice and from being the angel of storytelling became an organ-grinder, mocked, ignored and left outside, on the threshold of no-man's-land.

The relation between storyteller and childhood and their place in human destiny is a dominant theme in this film; both are symbolic of the possibility of the inner vision and will to believe, which precede creative growth. For Homer, the country of storytelling is the country of "hidden passes." "Why doesn't everyone see from childhood, the passes, the doors and crevices on the ground and above in the sky? If everyone saw them, there would be a history without murder or war." Or, as Pope Pius XII described it, the problem with the modern world is that it is no longer conscious of the presence of angels. For Jung, the problem is that we have lost our belief in spirit.

> For a long time the spirit, and the sufferings of the spirit, were positive values and the things most worth striving for in our peculiar Christian culture. Only in the course of the nineteenth century, when spirit began to degenerate into intellect, did a reaction set in against the unbearable dominance of intellectualism, and this led to the unpardonable mistake of confusing intellect with spirit and blaming the latter for the misdeeds of the former. The intellect does indeed do harm to the soul when it dares to possess itself of the heritage of the spirit. It is in no way fitted to do this, for spirit is something higher than intellect since it embraces the latter and includes the feelings as well. It is a guiding principle of life that strives towards superhuman, shining heights.[19]

If we lose the storyteller—our belief in angels and spirit—if we can no longer look through the hidden passes and crevices, we lose the child—our potential for growth and wholeness. Jung, too, deplores this possibility:

> In every adult there lurks a child—an eternal child, something that is always becoming, is never completed, and calls for unceasing care, attention, and education. That is the part of the human personality which wants to develop and become whole. But the man of today is far indeed from this wholeness.[20]

> Consciousness hedged about by psychic powers, sustained or threatened or deluded by them, is the age-old experience of mankind. This experience has projected itself into the archetype of the child, which expresses man's wholeness. The "child" is all that is abandoned and exposed and at the same time divinely powerful; the insignificant, dubious beginning, and the triumphal end. The "eternal child" in man is an indescribable experience, an incongruity, a handicap, and a divine prerogative; an imponderable that determines the ultimate worth or worthlessness of a personality.[21]

Homer considers giving up but decides finally that he will not give up. In the last scenes of the film, while Cassiel watches from his perch on the wings of the colossal statue of the Victory angel, Homer walks toward the Berlin wall, seeking his listeners who, he knows, are searching for him. "Name for me the men, women, and children who will look for me . . . me, their storyteller, their spiritual guide—because they need me more than anything in the world. We have embarked!" Written in the sky are the words that both end the film and promise a new beginning . . . "TO BE CONTINUED."

✪✪✪✪✪✪✪

The second approach to *Wings of Desire* is through an exploration of it as myth that has affinities with Jung's myth of meaning. What is that myth? We have seen that without the storyteller we are unable to find our myths, those that speak to the child in us and so help us to grow creatively. The reiterated questions of the child in this film,

> Why am I me, and not you?
> Why am I here, and why not there?
> When did time begin, and where does space end?
> Isn't life under the sun just a dream?

express the spiritual questions of our time. "Primitive man," Jung says, "is no puzzle to himself. The question 'What is man?' is the question that man has always kept until last. . . . This experience has projected itself into the archetype of the child, which expresses man's wholeness."[22]

The child paves the way for a future change of personality. In the individuation process, it anticipates the integration that comes from the synthesis of conscious and unconscious elements. It is therefore a unifying symbol which unites the opposites, a mediator, bringer of healing, "one who makes whole."

Jung sees in human consciousness a capacity for transformation that gives us an indispensable place in the spiritual world. Our consciousness has been creative in both the evolution and differentiation of archetypal god-images, and gives meaning to the world. In a letter to Erich Neumann in 1959, Jung says: "Without the reflecting consciousness of man the world is a gigantic meaningless machine, for as far as we know man is the only creature that can discover 'meaning.'"[23] It is only with the development of our myths and projections that the gods have evolved. We never, says Aniela Jaffé, find a revelation of the godhead in its totality; but without myth man becomes sick, neurotic. For Jung, psychoneurosis was the suffering of a soul which had not discovered its meaning. To find one's myth means to find meaning; and meaning has curative power. The crisis of modern times for Western man is due to the failure of the Christian myth to evolve. The Christian myth has become mute, Jung declared, and if evolution is to proceed, new myths—with new meaning—would have to be found. Jung's answer to that problem was a myth of meaning in terms of an "answer to Job."

It is in the language of analytic psychology that Jung, another storyteller, brings his contribution to the Judaic-Christian myth. In this answer to Job, divine incarnation and the evolution of humanity merge, leaving open the unfolding both of human consciousness of Self and that of the godhead. The decisive transformation occurred, Jung tells us, with the New Testament message that God became incarnated in Jesus and took on the limitations of human life. As Jung sees it, this was God's answer to Job; incarnation was His way of rectifying the situation of His own unconsciousness and His injustice to Job.

From a psychological standpoint, moreover, the Self is an archetypal symbol of the god image; hence divine incarnation is at the same time god image and a symbol of human individuation and evolution.

In *Was C. G. Jung a Mystic?* Aniela Jaffé describes this duality—the individuation of man and the incarnation of the divine—as the same event expressed in different languages and from two different perspectives. In Jung's conception, she says, the incarnation of God is not yet completed with Christ's incarnation, since Christ was more divine than human and without sin. To complete that process, Jaffé says, incarnation would have to be realized in the ordinary creature, man. She adds, "With such a consciousness, or with the more complete incarnation, the way is prepared for a new stage in the individuation of mankind."[24]

Jung describes this process in *Answer to Job*.

> The future indwelling of the Holy Ghost in man amounts to a continuing incarnation of God. Christ, as the begotten son of God and pre-existing mediator, is a first-born and a divine paradigm which will be followed by further incarnations of the Holy Ghost in the empirical man.[25]

The celebration of Marion and Damiel of the new image they are creating contributes to that plan. From this perspective, where individuation is the realization of the divine in man, the incarnation of Jesus, described in *Answer to Job*, can be interpreted as initiating an exodus of spiritual beings, in which Damiel is following an impeccable example. Within that context, the myth in *Wings of Desire* is a reinforcement and continuation of Jung's myth.

Jung's story does not end here, however. The meaning we project through our myths is still *our* meaning. With his account of synchronicity, however, Jung the storyteller looks into the "cracks and crevices" to discover something more. *Wings of Desire* left the unseen, underlying matrix of meaning—of the cosmos, the angels, evolution—haunting the film, without offering any explanation. But it also left open the hint that an answer might be found if we keep alive the impulse to look through the hidden passes and crevices. Synchronicity provides a crevice through which we might look for that meaning.

Well aware that his introduction of the concept of synchronicity would provoke controversy, Jung appealed to the "open-mindedness and good will" of the reader. He acknowledged that there could be no question of a complete description and explanation of such complicated phenomena and limited himself to the attempt to open up that field which, however obscure, was nevertheless of great importance. Jung defined synchronicity as meaningful coincidences or acausal orderedness.

> Meaningful coincidences are thinkable as pure chance. But the more they multiply and the greater and more exact the correspondence is, the more their probability sinks and their unthinkability increases, until they can no longer be regarded as pure chance but for lack of a causal explanation, have to be thought of as meaningful arrangements.[26]

The problem is not due to the mere fact that the cause is unknown, but that it is not even thinkable. Jung saw synchronicity not as competing with causality but as a category to be added to the triad, time, space, and causality; and it is through this category of synchronicity that we find the crevices and openings that suggest hidden meaning. Marion *knows* she will meet the someone she is looking for. Damiel *knows* that, although the circus has left, he will see Marion that evening. That knowledge is not justified through causal reasoning.

Jung accounts for the peculiar orderedness of synchronous events through his description of the archetype as "psychoid." He chose the term "psychoid" to indicate that the nature of the archetype *per se*, deep in the collective unconscious, is "psyche-like," although it cannot, *qua* archetype, be known by consciousness. Its presence as an instinctual pattern of behavior can be inferred, however, through its capacity to produce archetypal representations. Since the unconscious is not limited by space and time, archetypal interaction is not restricted to causal connection; therefore, acausal connections which are meaningful—although causally inexplicable—can be interpreted as connections through archetypal equivalences.

Archetypal equivalences represent, Jung says, a special instance of randomness or chance. He describes synchronicity in the narrow sense as particular instances of general acausal orderedness—meaning by the "narrow sense" that they express those equivalences of psychic and physical processes which we encounter as unique events in our lives. If our experience of synchronicity in the form of meaningful coincidences, as for instance, thinking of a friend we haven't seen in ten years on the very day we receive a letter from him, is only one instance of *general* acausal orderedness, then the idea of a whole matrix of meaning with the same (unknown to us) orderedness is suggested. The particular meaningful coincidences which we experience would then serve as the passes, crevices, chinks, through which we strain in order to gain a glimpse of that order—an underlying hidden matrix of meaning. This possibility, presumably, is what Jung had in mind with the following assertion. "It is man who creates meaning. Yet, given a view of the world that includes the unconscious, this statement too must be complemented by its opposite; the hypothesis of a meaning subsisting in itself and independent of man."[27] Synchronistic phenomena, and especially acausal extrasensory perceptions, are what led Jung to the inference of a transcendental meaning independent of consciousness.

Now we can see the consistency behind what seemed to be two opposing views: the first, that we project our own meanings and interpretations and find our own myths to remain healthy; and the second, that there is an acausal orderedness, a matrix of meaning, which is independent of us. According to Jung, the two are not inconsistent, we have intimations and intuitions from unknown sources. Fears, moods, plans and hopes befall us from invisible causes. In *Memories, Dreams, Reflections*, he says: "We must face the fact that our world, with its time, space, and causality, relates to another order of things lying behind or beneath it, in which neither 'here and there' nor 'earlier and later' are of importance."[28] Thus our creative myths incorporate our intimations from an unknown source and lend a transcendental grounding which, though never more than "intimations," yet provide us with inner confirmation of our doubts. As long as our myths bridge that discontinuity, no conflict exists between the causal and acausal orders. "The need for mythic statements is satisfied when we frame a view of the world which adequately explains the meaning of human existence in the cosmos, a view which springs from our psychic wholeness, from the co-operation between conscious and unconscious."[29] The myths that work for us are those that incorporate both worlds through a meaningful story which leads us to a constant transcending of ourselves toward a goal. For Jung it was individuation, the wholeness of the Self. Damiel described that wholeness which he and Marion created as "an immortal common image."

Wings of Desire began with a panoramic glimpse of contemporary life—scenes of depressed, anxiety-ridden crowds on the subway, isolated and preoccupied people sitting alone in their apartments, economically depressed extras waiting patiently for hours on the film set, this dreary present made even more gloomy through the series of flashback scenes of World War II and the presence of actors in the uniforms of the SS. All this becomes a very graphic description of what Jung called "the spiritual problem of modern man." But, "danger itself fosters the rescuing power."[30] Benevolent forces watch over this world and take care to preserve the storyteller, whose presence is crucial for the evolution of humankind. Although he wavers momentarily, the storyteller does not give up, refinds his mission, and sets off to find his listeners, those who are seeking him. He knows that it is his myths which keep childhood alive in humanity, and it is the child who brings a creative future into being.

We only half understand a man, Jung says, when we know how everything in him came into being. But life does not have only a yesterday, it has also a tomorrow. To understand fully, we need to add to the yesterday the beginnings of tomorrow. The film *Wings of Desire* is itself a myth of new beginnings, through a benevolent projection of a new childhood for humanity. And for those beginnings we need the vitality and optimism of the child who still looks through the cracks and crevices for answers to its questions:

Why am I me, and not you?
Why am I here, and not there?
When did time begin, and where does space end?
Isn't life under the sun just a dream?

Notes

1. Carl Gustav Jung, *The Sprit in Man, Art, and Literature*, trans. R. F. C. Hull (Princeton: Princeton University Press, 1971), 95.

2. Quotations from the dialogue in this film are taken from two sources: 1) a transcription of the English subtitles (transcribed for me by Bill Spencer), and 2) *Les Ailes du Désir*, Peter Handke and Wim Wenders (Le Chesnay, France: Editions Jade-Flammarion, 1989). The French translation from the original German is by Dominique Petit and Bernard Eisenschlitz.

3. Carl Gustav Jung, *C. G. Jung Speaking*, McGuire and R. F. C. Hull, eds. (Princeton: Princeton University Press, 1977), 68. This quotation is taken from the reprinting of an article published in *Hearst's International Cosmopolitan* for April 1934, supposedly by C. G. Jung, with the subheading, "A famous ultra-modern psychologist finds that the supreme need of man's spirit is met by the ancient spirit of Easter." Jung, however, had written to an American correspondent on April 21, 1934: "By the way, my so-called article in the *Cosmopolitan Magazine* was an interview with a reporter and not an article written by myself. I have not even seen a copy of it." I cite this article because, granting the above, the quotation in question is consistent with what Jung has written in other articles, especially in "The Spiritual Problem of Modern Man."

4. Jung, *C. G. Jung Speaking*, 377.

5. Carl Gustav Jung, *Psychological Reflections*, eds. Jolande Jacobi and R. F. C. Hull (Princeton: Princeton University Press, 1973), 268.

6. Jung, *Psychological Reflections*, 270.

7. Gustav Davidson, *A Dictionary of Angels* (Toronto: Collier-Macmillan Canada, 1967), 82.

8. Davidson, *A Dictionary of Angels*, 94-95.

9. Davidson, *A Dictionary of Angels*, xvii.

10. Davidson, *A Dictionary of Angels*, 349.
11. Jung, *C. G. Speaking*, 301.
12. Jung, *C. G. Speaking*, 413.
13. Jung, *C. G. Speaking*, 420.
14. Jung, *Psychological Reflections*, 308.
15. Jung, *Modern Man in Search of a Soul*, 219.
16. Carl Gustav Jung, *Modern Man in Search of a Soul*, trans. Dell and Baynes (New York: Harvest Book, Harcourt, Brace and World, 1933), 220.
17. Jung, *Psychological Reflections*, 296.
18. Peter Handke and Wim Wenders, *Les Ailes du Désir* (Le Chesnay, France: Editions Jade-Flammarion, 1989), back cover (my translation).
19. Jung, *Psychological Reflections*, 254.
20. Jung, *Psychological Reflections*, 311.
21. Carl Gustav Jung, *Collected Works* vol. 9.1, trans. R. F. C. Hull (Princeton: Princeton University Press, 1968), 178-79.
22. Carl Gustav Jung, *Psyche and Symbol*, ed. Violet S. de Laszlo (Garden City: Doubleday Anchor Books, Doubleday and Company, 1958), 144.
23. Aniela Jaffé, *The Myth of Meaning*, trans. R. F. C. Hull (New York: Penguin Books, 1975), 140.
24. Jaffé, *Was C. G. Jung a Mystic?*, trans. Diana Dachler and Fiona Cairns; ed. Robert Hinshaw, assisted by Gary Massey and Henriette Wagner (Einsiedeln: Daimon Verlag, 1989), 87.
25. Carl Gustav Jung, *Collected Works* vol. 11, trans. R. F. C. Hull (Princeton: Princeton University Press, 1973), 432.
26. Carl Gustav Jung, *Synchronicity*, trans. R. F. C. Hull (Princeton: Princeton University Press, 1973), 102-3.
27. Jaffé, *The Myth of Meaning*, 150.
28. Carl Gustav Jung, *Memories, Dreams, Reflections* (New York: Random House, 1961), 305.
29. Jung, *Memories, Dreams, Reflections*, 340.
30. Jung, *Modern Man in Search of a Soul*, 220.

BIBLIOGRAPHY

Adlon, Eleonore, and Percy Adlon. *Bagdad Cafe* (film script). Los Angeles: Island Pictures, pelemele FILM GmbH production, 1987.
Allende, Isabel. *The House of the Spirits*. Trans. Magda Bogin. New York: Bantam Books, 1986.
Bolen, Jean Shenoda. *The Tao of Psychology*. San Francisco: Harper and Row, 1979.
Coward, H. *Jung and Eastern Thought*. Albany: State University of New York Press, 1985.
Czuczka, George. *Imprints of the Future*. Washington: Daimon, 1987.
Davidson, Gustav. *A Dictionary of Angels*. Toronto: Collier-Macmillan Canada, 1967.
de Castillejo, Irene Claremont. *Knowing Woman*. New York: Harper Colophon Books, 1973.
Dostoyevsky, Fyodor. *A Raw Youth*. Trans. Constance Garnett. New York: Dial Press, 1947.
———. *The Brothers Karamazov*. Trans. Constance Garnett. New York: Modern Library, 1950.
———. *Crime and Punishment*. New York: Modern Library, 1950.
———. *The Idiot*. Trans. David Magarshack. London: Penguin Classics, 1955.
Edinger, E. *Ego and Archetype*. Baltimore: G. P. Putnam, 1972.
Handke, Peter, and Wim Wenders. *Les Ailes du Désir*. Traduction française: Dominique Petit et Bernard Eisenschitz. Le Chesnay: Editions Jade-Flammarion, 1989.
Harding, Esther. *The i and the Not i*. Princeton: Princeton University Press, 1973.

Jacobi, Jolande. *Complex/Archetype/Symbol in the Psychology of C. G. Jung*. Trans. Ralph Manheim. Princeton: Princeton University Press, 1971.

———. *The Psychology of C. G. Jung*. Trans. Ralph Manheim. New Haven: Yale University Press, 1943.

———. *The Way of Individuation*. Trans. R. F. C. Hall. New York: New American Library, 1983.

Jaffé, Aniela. *From the Life and Work of C. G. Jung*. Trans. R. F. C. Hall. New York: Harper & Row, 1971.

———. *The Myth of Meaning in the Work of C. G. Jung*. Trans. R. F. C. Hall. New York: Penguin Books, 1971.

———. *Was C. G. Jung a Mystic?* Trans. Diana Dachler and Fiona Cairns; edited by Robert Hinshaw, assisted by Gary Massey and Henriette Wagner. Einsiedeln: Daimon Verlag, 1989.

Jung, C. G. *Analytical Psychology*. New York: Random House, 1970.

———. *The Collected Works of C. G. Jung*. Eds. H. Read, M. Fordham and G. Adler, trans. R. F. C. Hull. Princeton: Princeton University Press, 1953-83.

———. *C. G. Jung Speaking: Interviews and Encounters*. Eds. W. McGuire and R. F. C. Hull. Princeton: Princeton University Press, 1977.

———. *Memories, Dreams, Reflections*. Trans. Richard Winston and Chara Winston; ed. Aniela Jaffé. New York: Random House, 1961.

———. *Modern Man in Search of a Soul*. Trans. W. S. Dell and Cary F. Baynes. New York: Harcourt Brace and World, 1933.

———. *Nietzsche's Zarathustra*. Notes of the seminar given in 1934-39. Ed. James L. Jarett. Princeton: Princeton University Press, 1988.

———. *On the Nature of the Psyche*. Trans. R. F. C. Hall. New Jersey: Princeton University Press, 1960.

———. *Psyche and Symbol*. Ed. Violet S. de Laszlo. Garden City: Doubleday Anchor Books, Doubleday and Company, 1958.

———. *Psychological Reflections*. Eds. J. Jacobi and R. F. C. Hull. Princeton: Princeton University Press, 1974.

———. *Psychology and Religion*. New Haven: Yale University Press, 1966.

———. *Synchronicity: An Acausal Connecting Principle*. Trans. R. F. C. Hall. Princeton: Princeton University Press, 1973.

———. *Two Essays on Analytical Psychology*. Trans. R. F. C. Hall. Cleveland: World Publishing, 1967.

———. *The Undiscovered Self*. New York: The New American Library, 1957, 1958.

Jung, C. G. and Marie-Louise von Franz. *Man and His Symbols*. Ed. Carl G. Jung and Marie-Louise von Franz; Coordinating Editor John Freeman. New York: Dell Publishing, 1973.

Kaufman, Walter, ed. *Existentialism from Dostoyevsky to Sartre*. New York: New American Library, 1957.

Kazantzakis, Nikos. *Zorba the Greek*. Trans. Carl Wildman. New York: Simon & Schuster, 1953.

Kierkegaard, Sören. *Stages on Life's Way*. Trans. Walter Lowrie. New York: Schocken Books, 1967.

Laing, R. D. *The Divided Self*. New York: Penguin Books, 1965.

Leonard, Linda Schierse. *The Wounded Woman*. Athens: Ohio University Press, 1982.

Neumann, Erich. *Art and the Creative Unconscious*. Trans. Ralph Manheim. Princeton: Princeton University Press, 1959.

———. *Depth Psychology and a New Ethic*. Boston: Shambhala Publications, 1990.

Nietzsche, Friedrich. *The Gay Science*. Trans. Walter Kaufmann. New York: Random House, 1974.

Ostrowski-Sachs, Margaret. *From Conversations with C. G. Jung*. Trans. Margareta Marburg, Dr. C. Gattegno and Daniel H. Wheeler. Zürich: Juris Druck + Verlag, 1971.

Shawn, Wallace and André Gregory. *My Dinner With André, A Screen Play for the Film by Louis Malle*. New York: Grove Press, 1981.

Spiegelman, J. Marvin and Mokusen Miyuki. *Buddhism and Jungian Psychology*. Phoenix: Falcon Press, 1985.

Ulanov, A. B. *The Feminine in Jungian Psychology and in Christian Theology*. Evanston: Northwestern University Press, 1971.

Von Franz, Marie-Louise. *C. G. Jung: His Myth in Our Time*. Trans. William H. Kennedy. New York: G. P. Putnam, 1975.

———. *Dreams*. Boston: Shambhala Publication, 1990.

———. *Jung's Typology*. Trans. H. G. Baynes. New York: Spring Publications, 1971.

Wehr, Demaris S. *Jung and Feminism*. Boston: Beacon Press, 1987.

Whitmont, Edward C. *The Symbolic Quest*. New York: Harper & Row, 1973.

INDEX

Angel, 6, 97-110, 112
Anima, 4-5, 9, 19, 29-32, 39-40, 48-50
Animus, 4-5
Answer to Job, 111-12
Archetype, 4-5, 9, 44, 49, 85-86, 110-11, 113; child, 110-11; religious, 44, 86

Bolen, Jean, 60
Book of Job, 99
Brothers Karamazov, The, 26, 84, 86-87, 90, 92-93
Buddha, 21, 25
Buddhist beliefs, 21
Buddhist compassion, 20
Buddhist priest, 75
Buddhist Zen Masters, 24-25

Christ, 73, 86, 112
Christian Myth, 111
Compulsion, 43-44, 47, 52, 85
Creativity, 60, 64, 74

Davidson, Gustav, 103
de Castillejo, Irene, 57, 64

Depth Psychology and a New Ethic, 75
Devil, 18, 23-24, 87
Dictionary of Angels, 103
Divided Self, The, 7
Dostoyevsky, Fyodor, 6, 48, 52, 54, 83-86, 90, 93-94
Dreams, 6-7, 9, 20, 46-48, 52-54, 83-84, 86-94, 98, 100-101, 111, 114-15; big, 6, 83, 89, 90; compensating function of, 83, 91; prophetic, 90

Evolution, 4, 6, 9, 75, 99, 104-5, 111-12, 114; creative, 23; spiritual, 3

God, 1, 16-18, 20, 23-26, 45, 47, 52, 87-89, 91, 93-94, 100, 103, 106, 111-12; death of, 1, 91; incarnation of, 112; return of, 91

Idiot, The, 84
Inferior Function, 16-17, 63

Jacobi, Jolande, 14
Jaffé, Aniela, 75, 111-12
Jung's Typology, 24, 63

Kazantzakis, Nikos, 13-15
Kierkegaard, Sören, 9, 87
Knowing Woman, 64

Man and His Symbols, 19
Memories, Dreams, Reflections, 114
Myth, 6, 75, 99, 101, 111-12, 114-15
Myth of Meaning in the Work of C. G. Jung, 75

Neumann, Erich, 8, 75, 111
Nietzsche, Friedrich, 1, 4
Nihilism, 1-2, 45, 48, 50, 53, 89-90

Ostrowski-Sachs, Margaret, 29

Persona, 37, 39
Projection, 8-9, 30-31, 48, 50, 62, 65, 72, 111, 115
Psychological types; function differences: feeling, 5, 15-16, 19-21, 45-46, 90; intuition, 15, 90; sensation, 15, 20, 24; thinking, 5, 15-17, 20, 45-46; attitude differences: extraversion, 5, 15, 85; extraverted type, 15-16, 62, 65; introversion, 5, 15, 62, 85; introverted type, 62

Rainmaker, 6, 57-58, 60, 63-68
Rationality, 44, 52, 90
Raw Youth, A, 90

Rebirth, 54, 63, 83-89, 92-94, 106; *see* spiritual rebirth
Relativism, 50, 73, 89
Report to Greco, 13-14, 25
Repression, 30, 39

Science, 79, 97, 100
Self, 2, 4, 7-8, 14, 30, 48, 52-53, 64, 86, 93, 107, 111-12, 114
Shadow, 5, 8, 15, 17-18, 38-39, 48, 50-51, 62, 87; of God, 1, 45
Spirit, 2, 6, 8-9, 13, 17, 21-23, 63, 71, 75, 89-90, 92, 99-102, 105, 108-10; of the age, 80; *see* spirit and matter
Spirit and Matter, 6, 99, 108
Spiritual emptiness, vacuum, 1, 2, 72
Spiritual isolation, 106
Spiritual forms, 73, 80, 85
Spiritual problem of modern man, 2, 6, 72, 79-80, 99, 101, 107, 114
Spiritual rebirth, transformation, 3, 53-54, 63, 84, 86, 88, 93;
Spiritual suffering, 104, 110
Strada, La, 7
Suffering, 13, 20, 22, 24-25, 34, 44, 52, 85-86, 104, 111
Symbol, 6-7, 19, 22-23, 37, 52, 54, 83-86, 99, 112; unifying, 111
Symbolic images, 84, 90
Symbolic messages, 2, 4, 44, 83
Symbolism, 8, 54, 98, 106
Synchronicity, 75, 112-13

Transformation, 3-4, 6, 8-9, 14, 20-21, 30, 39, 44, 54, 60, 63,

65, 76, 79, 83-84, 86, 93-94, 106, 111-12; *see* spiritual rebirth

Two Essays on Analytical Psychology, 14, 62

Unconscious, 2-4, 8, 30, 34, 43-44, 49, 54, 62, 72, 74-76, 78-80, 83, 87, 91, 94, 100-101, 106, 113-14; communal, 74, 77-78; fascination with, 2, 73, 80; personal, 5, 87; *see* projection, *see* shadow

Undiscovered Self, The, 93

Von Franz, Marie-Louise, 16, 19, 24-25, 30, 63

Was C. G. Jung a Mystic? 112

Wenders, Wim, 109

ABOUT THE AUTHOR

Phyllis Berdt Kenevan, Ph.D., was a Fulbright Scholar at the Sorbonne in Paris and also spent a semester at the Jung Institute in Küsnacht, Switzerland. Now Professor Emerita, she was a member of the philosophy department at the University of Colorado for 36 years during which time she was a co-director of the honors program and director of the study abroad program at Bordeaux. She has published articles in books and journals on both Jungian psychology and existential philosophy. She lives in Boulder, Colorado.